American Interests,
American Purpose

THE WASHINGTON PAPERS

... intended to meet the need for an authoritative, yet prompt, public appraisal of the major developments in world affairs.

President, CSIS: David M. Abshire

Series Editor: Walter Laqueur

Director of Publications: Nancy B. Eddy

Managing Editor: Donna R. Spitler

MANUSCRIPT SUBMISSION

The Washington Papers and Praeger Publishers welcome inquiries concerning manuscript submissions. Please include with your inquiry a curriculum vitae, synopsis, table of contents, and estimated manuscript length. Manuscripts must be between 120–200 double-spaced typed pages. All submissions will be peer reviewed. Submissions to *The Washington Papers* should be sent to *The Washington Papers*; The Center for Strategic and International Studies; 1800 K Street NW; Suite 400; Washington, DC 20006. Book proposals should be sent to Praeger Publishers; One Madison Avenue; New York NY 10010.

The Washington Papers/139

American Interests, American Purpose

Moral Reasoning and U.S. Foreign Policy

George Weigel

Foreword by Max M. Kampelman

Published with The Center for
Strategic and International Studies
Washington, D.C.

PRAEGER

New York
Westport, Connecticut
London

Library of Congress Cataloging-in-Publication Data

Weigel, George,
  American interests, American purpose.

  (Washington papers, 0278-937X ; 139)
  "Published with the Center for Strategic and
International Studies, Washington, D.C."
  Bibliography: p.
  Includes index.
  1. United States – Foreign relations – 1945–   –
Moral and ethical aspects. I. Center for Strategic
and International Studies (Washington, D.C.) II. Title.
III. Series.
JX1417.W4   1989   172′.4′0973   89-3564
ISBN 0-275-93335-0 (alk. paper)
ISBN 0-275-93336-9 (pbk. alk. paper)

Library of Congress Catalog Card Number: 89-3564
ISBN: 0-275-93335-0 (HB)
       0-275-93336-9 (PB)

First published in 1989

Praeger Publishers, One Madison Avenue, New York, NY 10010
A division of Greenwood Press, Inc.

Printed in the United States of America

For Carl Gershman
and
Richard Schifter —
advocates for peace and freedom

Contents

Foreword   ix

About the Author   xiii

Acknowledgments   xv

Preface   xvii

Summary   xxi

1. Exorcising Wilson's Ghost—Morality and
   Foreign Policy in America's Third Century   1

   A Question of Roots   2
   The Niebuhrian Sensibility   5
   Situating the New Argument   7
   Focusing the Debate   11
   Beyond Circularity   16

2. A Question of Honor—The War Novels of
   Evelyn Waugh   18

   The Procrustean Bed of Bureaucracy   24
   The Compromise with Totalitarianism   29
   The Choice for Honor   34

3. **Nuclear Deterrence and the Common Morality**   **37**

    Beyond the Bernardin Barrier   39
    Attending to History   43
    "Common Morality" and Deterrence   46
    Disputed Questions   51
    On Not Ignoring the Radical   57

4. **Ethics Meets Strategy: U.S. Foreign Policy and the Democratic Prospect**   **59**

    The Case for Democracy: Moral Considerations   61
    The Case for Democracy: Empirical Considerations   65
    The Case for Democracy: Strategic Considerations   71
    Advices and Cautions   73
    Beyond Evangelism   76

Notes   79

Index   93

Foreword

When the revered Reinhold Niebuhr wrote about the "Children of Light and the Children of Darkness," he was reflecting an ancient understanding that is deeply embedded in the Jewish tradition from which I come. According to that tradition, the struggle between the *yaitzer hatov* (that which is Godlike and good in the heart and soul and being of man) and the *yaitzer hara* (our inclinations to evil) defines the human condition. This human characteristic obviously reflects itself in the institutions man creates. In the course of public life, in law and in diplomacy, I have had many opportunities to watch that struggle express itself in the political process.

George Weigel's work is an impressive attempt to think about the relationship between moral reasoning and foreign policy in a persistently conflicted world: a world in which the *yaitzer hatov* and the *yaitzer hara* are in perennial contest. But George Weigel should not be understood as one of the terrible simplifiers whose quick and easy answers to the dilemmas of the policymaker have made some realists skeptical about the very notion that U.S. foreign policy should be guided by moral norms. Rather, George Weigel's is an argument against antinomies: he resists, with intellectual rigor, the temptation to sunder peace and freedom, realism and idealism, national interest and national purpose. In doing so, he reminds us that moral reasoning, a strength, should not be confused with moralism, and he asks that we recover the idea, central to the political tradition of the West since Aristotle, that prudence is the greatest of virtues in public life.

By "prudence," George Weigel means that moral skill which allows us to bring moral norms and the facts of international public life into a creative, rather than destructive, tension. That concern is all the more welcome today, in that the past 20 years of foreign policy debate have taught us many hard lessons about the temptation to moralism in the policy debate (so manifestly evident during the Vietnam period). Conversely, we have also learned that any successful U.S. foreign policy must be one the American people understand to reflect the deepest values on which our own national experiment rests. At the close of the 1980s, I see hopeful signs that the policy community is, once again, willing to engage in the debate to which George Weigel has devoted such careful attention: the debate over moral *reasoning* and U.S. foreign policy.

What would a healthy debate in this field look like?

It would be characterized by reason and informed opinion, rather than by passion married to ignorance.

It would be ecumenical, engaging the full range of religious and ethical traditions at play in our country, rather than narrow and sectarian.

It would acknowledge the special character of the United States as a nation built on the idea and value of human freedom, but it would do so without hubris.

It would avoid the temptation to messianism, while at the same time avoiding messianism's mirror image, cynicism.

Such a debate, were it to unfold, would help set standards, not simply for scholarly discussion, but for policy-formation and the definition of America's multiple responsibilities and relationships in the world.

American Interests, American Purpose is an important

contribution to the possibility of such a new debate by a young scholar who stands in the tradition of Reinhold Niebuhr and John Courtney Murray, but who is stretching that tradition of Christian realism in new and promising directions. George Weigel's work deserves the closest attention of moral theorists and policymakers alike.

Max M. Kampelman
Former Counselor of the U.S. Department of State
and Head of U.S. Delegation,
Negotiations on Nuclear and Space Arms

About the Author

George Weigel, a Roman Catholic theologian, is the
president of the Ethics and Public Policy Center in Washington, D.C. Educated at St. Mary's Seminary and University in Baltimore and the University of St. Michael's Col-
lege in Toronto, he was a 1984–1985 fellow of the Woodrow
Wilson International Center for Scholars and has served as
a consultant to members of Congress, officials of the executive branch, and religious leaders on issues of ethics and
U.S. foreign policy.

Acknowledgments

Conversations with Robert Andrews, Peter Berger, Alberto Coll, William Douglas, James Turner Johnson, John Langan, S. J., Ralph McInerny, Richard John Neuhaus, Michael Novak, Robert Pickus, and R. James Woolsey helped shape some of the arguments that follow. Belated thanks, too, to my Scottish uncle-in-law, G. Stanley Gimson, Q. C., who introduced me to Waugh's *Sword of Honor* trilogy.

Amy L. Sherman, my colleague in the work of the James Madison Foundation, prepared the final manuscript with her usual competence and good cheer.

Brad Roberts and Donna Spitler of the Center for Strategic and International Studies suggested that I undertake this project, and I am grateful for their importunings, counsel, and friendship.

An earlier version of chapter 1 appeared in *The Washington Quarterly*; an earlier version of chapter 3 appeared in *Crisis*. Thanks to both of those journals for their invitations to write on these topics.

I dedicate this book to two friends whose admirable public service in the 1980s has demonstrated that moral concern and strategic sophistication can complement each other so that the national interest and the national purpose are both served: Carl Gershman, president of the National Endowment for Democracy, and Ambassador Richard Schifter, assistant secretary of state for human rights and humanitarian affairs in the second Reagan administration.

G. W.

Preface

"Morality-and-foreign-policy" is one of those topics that, to foreign policy realists, has an effect similar to that achieved by fingernails raked down a blackboard. On the other side of the polemical barricades, those typically characterized as "idealists" often conduct their controversies as a species of moral emoting, thereby confirming the realists' sense that normative issues have no place in the hard-boiled arena of world politics. Proponents on both sides of this debate have an unfortunate tendency to view their adversaries as idiots: either strategic idiots or moral idiots. This is not a happy circumstance for the American republic as it enters its third century under the Constitution of 1787.

Moreover, given the origins and nature of the American experiment in ordered liberty, and indeed given the nature of politics as that has been understood in the great tradition of the West since Aristotle, the topic simply will not go away. Politics *is* an extension of ethics, and so the real question for debate has to do, not with the fact, but with the quality, of the moral reasoning that is an integral part of America's unavoidable engagement with international public life.

This small volume is a modest attempt to raise the

quality of that encounter between the worlds of the policy-maker and the moral theorist.

Chapter 1 is a brief overview of the morality-and-foreign-policy debate in the United States, locating its modern misconstruction in the cultural Protestantism out of which Woodrow Wilson thought about these matters, and proposing that a different way of conceiving the "morality" side of the argument might lead us beyond the circularity that has too often characterized the debate.

Chapter 2 suggests that Evelyn Waugh's trilogy of novels on World War II offers important insights into the fundamental moral issues posed by the nature of modern war and by the rise of totalitarian politics in the twentieth century.

Chapter 3 takes up a hotly controverted topic of the 1980s: the ethics of nuclear deterrence. Contrary to the usual public perceptions, the attack on deterrence is now being mounted from the right as well as the left of the U.S. religious community. The substance of that critique, the insight it affords into the nature of moral reasoning on issues of foreign and defense policy, and a path beyond the present ethical logjam are explored in turn.

Finally, chapter 4 examines the moral claims of the world's democrats as they bear on the design and implementation of U.S. foreign policy. Religious activists persistently argue that a "preferential option for the poor" ought to shape America's action in the world. Is there a "preferential option for freedom" with a parallel, and perhaps even prior, claim to our attention? Can the moral case for U.S. support of the democratic revolution in world politics be completed by a persuasive empirical and strategic analysis? And if that were done, might it point a way ahead of the present left-right barricades in the debate over ethics and U.S. foreign policy? These questions are examined here.

Readers may come to the end of this small volume with a sense of dissatisfaction, thinking, Is this all there is to say on the matter of morality and foreign policy? Obviously, it is not. But if these four essays, which may be taken

as signposts driven into a peculiarly murky terrain, suggest that the argument over moral norms and U.S. foreign
policy is not necessarily circular, but has a perennial quality
that just might lead to a measure of prudential wisdom in
the conduct of our affairs, their purpose will have been
achieved.

Washington, D.C.

All Saints, 1988

Summary

American Interests, American Purpose explores a hardy perennial in the garden of American political controversy: the relationship between moral norms and U.S. foreign policy.

The book does not so much attempt to provide a theoretical framework for the ongoing morality-and-foreign-policy debate as to examine four different facets of an argument that just won't go away, the fond hopes of some policymakers and commentators notwithstanding.

Chapter 1 explores the skewing of the morality-and-foreign-policy debate occasioned by the cultural Protestant moralism that characterized Woodrow Wilson's approach to world politics. Here, author Weigel suggests that, contrary to the received wisdom on the subject, the basic issue for debate is not at the "policy" end of the discussion, but rather involves the more fundamental question, "What do you mean by morality or moral reasoning?"

Chapter 2 examines—through the literary lens of Evelyn Waugh's trilogy of novels on World War II—the pressures put on the foreign policy debate by the rise of modern totalitarianism.

Chapter 3 analyzes a new feature in an old debate. Liberal churchmen and moral theorists have often chafed under the sword of Damocles that is nuclear deterrence. Now, new contestants have entered the anti-deterrence lists: conservative moral theorists who claim to be operating according to the classic canons of the "common morality." Weigel examines and critiques their case, while warning that policymakers and commentators ignore the radical (of left or right) at their peril.

Chapter 4 sketches the moral, strategic, and empirical case for a U.S. foreign policy in which support for indigenous democratic forces throughout the world has a high priority. The Latin American theologies of liberation have made the phrase "preferential option for the poor" a staple in the argument over America's role in world affairs. Author Weigel argues that a "preferential option for freedom" provides a better moral and political context in which to approach the myriad problems of security, poverty, and tyranny in Second, Third, and Fourth World arenas.

American Interests,
American Purpose

1

Exorcising Wilson's Ghost— Morality and Foreign Policy in America's Third Century

As the United States enters its third century under the Constitution of 1787, few bets are as safe as a bet that issues of morality and foreign policy will continue to be argued with much heat, if not commensurate light, in our public life.

What ought the United States do in Central America? Is strategic defense a more morally acceptable means of security than deterrence maintained by the threat of mutual assured destruction? What responsibilities does the United States have for the cause of human rights in the world? What is a human right, for that matter? Do the world's democrats have a moral claim on U.S. support? And what happens when those claims abut other grave national security interests?

There is something quintessentially American about these, and similar, arguments. It is hard to imagine their equivalents arising on the Quai d'Orsay or in Whitehall — much less, one hardly needs to add, in Eduard Shevardnadze's staff meetings. They crop up with impressive regularity in our public discourse for any number of reasons — among them, that Americans are an incorrigibly religious people who, since the days of John Winthrop and Roger Williams, have brought their religious convictions and the moral norms they derive therefrom into the square where the public's business is contested. But the most critical reason that the morality-and-foreign-policy debate remains a hardy perennial in the garden of American political controversy has to do with the very nature of the American experiment itself.

A Question of Roots

Unlike other nations, whose roots lie in the soil of tribe, race, ethnicity, or language, the United States is a country whose casements rest on an idea. Thomas Jefferson expressed it succinctly in the Declaration of Independence – "All men are created equal." At Gettysburg, Abraham Lincoln described Jefferson's claim as a "proposition" that would always be tested by our public life. And here, argued the great Jesuit theologian John Courtney Murray, Lincoln was speaking with "conceptual propriety," for in philosophy a proposition is "the statement of a truth to be demonstrated."[1] Jefferson's definition of the "American proposition" has had, and continues to have, a pronounced effect on the conduct of America's business with the world. In that sense, Murray's notion of a continually tested proposition is validated by every morning's headlines.

Jefferson's claim was, of course, a moral claim. Its impact on U.S. foreign policy, for better and for worse, and often for both, derives from its universality. The Founding Fathers did not pledge their "lives, fortunes, and sacred honor" to a narrow claim ("All white, male, Protestant, English colonists living on the eastern seaboard of North America between the Atlantic Ocean and the Mississippi River are created equal") but to a simple, unequivocal, universal claim – All men are created equal. Moreover, the Declaration argued, this claim could be known by all men of good will. It did not derive from sectarian religious tradition, but from human nature itself. "Nature, and Nature's God" had created all men equal.

Thus, and from its inception, the American experiment was more than a matter of a new "is" in world affairs. The Founding Fathers asserted an "ought." Charles Krauthammer has made the connection between this "ought" and the distinctive character of American nationalism: "Our nationalism is unlike others, in that our very nationhood is bound up with and is meant to give expression to the idea of freedom."[2] That this morally based nationalism would have its effect on U.S. foreign policy was as certain a speculation as one could have made, even in the days of America's hemispheric isolation. Given the proper historical circumstances, Americans would have to deal with the world. And they would, inevitably, cast that encounter in terms that reflected their originating experience and continuing experiment.

No small part of our present difficulty with the morality and foreign policy debate derives from the historical circumstances in which that encounter took place in World War I. That it was Woodrow Wilson who first articulated the themes of America's entry as a great power onto the world stage has made an enormous difference. For Wilson embodied a specific form of American Protestant moral sensibility that has been the entry point for, as well as the chief defect of, the morality and foreign policy debate since April 1917.

Throughout the nineteenth century and well into the twentieth, the United States had a semi-established religion, what sociologist Peter Berger has described as *Kulturprotestantismus*.[3] This generalized Protestant religiosity carried with it a particular understanding of morality, traces of which can be found in artifacts ranging from the McGuffey readers to the League of Nations Charter and the Kellogg-Briand Treaty.

It was a morality that found the good in the will of God, rather than in human reason. As Murray once described it, *Kulturprotestantismus* taught that " . . . the good is good because God commands it; the evil is evil because God forbids it."[4] The notion that morality might have something to do with human reason and its capacity to discern moral norms from human nature and human history did not sit well.

The morality of *Kulturprotestantismus* likewise knew where one looked for the revelation of God's will: one looked to the Old and New Testaments. There was a fundamentalist current at play here. Scholarly biblical exegesis was not of much moment. One took the Biblical texts as they stood and applied them to the policy arena in a kind of one-to-one correspondence.

Wilson's morality also set great store by one's intentions. As Murray put it, "It set primary and controlling value on a sincerity of interior motives; what matters is not what you do but why you do it."[5] This led rather easily to a form of extreme moral idealism, which taught that the motive of love that ought to inform one's dealings with one's fellows could be applied, forthwith, to relations between organized political communities. And thus individualism was a fourth distinctive element in the moral sensibility of *Kulturprotestantismus*: standards of Christian perfection applicable to the individual could also be applied to the behavior of states. One could hope for, work for, and indeed expect the day when there would be no "moral problems" for domestic or international society, which blessed condition would automatically obtain if and when all men loved their neighbors.

This "older morality," as Murray was wont to call it, may have been marginally useful in providing rhetorical grease for America's sidestep into world politics. But it did little to illuminate those politics, and still less to provide moral standards for policy formulation. Its failure, though, should not be attributed to the fact that the world is an infinitely messy place, vastly plural in its religious, ethical, and ideological understandings and commitments, and thus constructed in a way that no moral norm could possibly be relevant to the design and conduct of U.S. foreign policy. Rather, the true fault lay in the concept of morality that was embedded in *Kulturprotestantismus* and that can be aptly described as Wilsonian moral*ism*. The deepest question to be addressed did not lie on the policy side of the morality and foreign policy dialectic. It lay on the first side of the equation. The priority question was, "What do we mean by 'morality'?"

The Niebuhrian Sensibility

A first and important cut at answering this question from outside the boundaries of the liberal Protestant hegemony came in the work of Reinhold Niebuhr and other Christian realists. Niebuhr and colleagues such as John C. Bennett argued in the 1930s that liberal Protestant moralism was utterly incapable of guiding the conduct of foreign policy in the face of modern totalitarianism. Rather, the social ethicist had to recover a classic Christian understanding: that the Kingdom of God would not be a work of human hands. In this world as it is, Christian theology and social theory had to consider the irreducible facts of tragedy, irony, and pathos in the human condition. To attempt blithely to transcend these facts of life in a fallen world, as Niebuhr believed Wilsonian moralism and Protestant liberalism did, was not only political folly; it was a corruption of Christian understandings of—in the classic images—the world, the flesh, and the devil. In the very first chapter of his seminal book, *Moral Man and Immoral Society*, Niebuhr stated flatly that "the dream of perpetual peace and brotherhood for human society will never be fully realized." That did not mean, as many have misinterpreted, that society and politics were somehow outside the boundaries within which moral reason could operate. It did mean that social ethics was a distinctive enterprise, which ought not be confused with the ethics of interpersonal relationships. One did not think morally about dealing with Hitler in precisely the same way that one reasoned morally about dealing with Aunt Mary.

Niebuhr's great accomplishment, which shaped and

was shaped by his interaction with the anti-Communist liberal internationalism characteristic of Americans for Democratic Action in its original incarnation, was to nail this point down for a generation: the voluntarism, fundamentalism, and individualism of the older morality made a chaos of both public policy and Christian doctrine. But Niebuhr did not venture very far beyond this essential contribution, and he never sketched a calculus by which moral reason could be applied, through the mediating virtue of prudence, to the design and conduct of foreign policy.

This was John Courtney Murray's critique of Niebuhr. Murray welcomed Niebuhr's insistence that complexity was the inescapable hallmark of policy choice; that historical circumstances had to be taken seriously; that the consequences of one's actions must be factored into the calculus of moral reason and policy choice; and that human tendencies toward evil were a built-in part of the human condition, not to be removed by therapy or baptism. In short, Niebuhr had dealt a serious blow to that sentimentality which was the leitmotif of the older morality and a corrupting influence within it.

But Niebuhr had stopped too soon, Murray suggested. Niebuhr was correct to assert the distinctiveness of social ethics against the ethics of interpersonal relationships. But the problem posed by liberal Protestant individualism was, at bottom, a false problem, and Niebuhr's solution to it posed a new danger: to posit the distinction between social and interpersonal ethics without grounding both ethical tasks in the functions of human reason, and in reason's ability to apprehend moral norms through reflection on human nature and human history, raised the prospect of social ethics' simply dropping off the ledge of our public discourse.

Nor did the themes of irony, tragedy, and pathos, evocative as they were, provide much grist for a task that Murray deemed paramount: the creation of a public philosophy expressed in a mediating language that could cut across the pluralisms of Protestant-Catholic-Jewish and religious-secular in such a way that genuinely public moral argument, rather than public moral emoting, became possible in American political culture.

What Reinhold Niebuhr offered, in short, was a sensibility that ought to furnish one corner of the intellect of anyone who dared to enter the minefield called morality and foreign policy. But more than a Niebuhrian sensibility was needed, in Murray's judgment. One needed a natural law–based social ethic that recognized that society and the state had their own distinctive purposes, not be confused with private purposes. One needed an ethic that acknowledged the centrality of national interest in the conduct of foreign policy and was not embarrassed by it, but which related national interest to a larger scheme of national purpose by resolutely drawing the line at *raison d'état* as a possible criterion for action. One needed a social ethic that knew that power – the ability to achieve a common purpose – was the central reality at the heart of any organized community. One needed a structure of moral reasoning that could distinguish, normatively, between power and sheer violence, and that could relate the proportionate and discriminate use of limited armed force to the pursuit of peace, security, and freedom. One needed, finally, a method of casuistry that could dialetically engage moral norms with messy human situations through the mediation of the central political virtue of prudence, or practical wisdom. One-to-one correspondences – between scriptural texts or moral norms, and the exigencies of policy – should be held frankly suspect, and precisely on moral grounds. Moral reasoning was not a set of how-to-do-it instructions that might be followed by any dolt; it was a matter of endless argument, research, reflection, more argument, and empirical testing.

Situating the New Argument

How does this question stand, as we enter America's third century? And beyond the possible fascinations of intellectual history, why should those concerned with the day-to-day dilemmas of power care, anyway?

The second question is answered simply, if sharply, by recognizing that the concept of value-free judgment in politics is an absurdity. There are no value-free judgments, no ethical free lunches. Every political judgment involves a calculus, usually inarticulate, involving questions of "ought" as well as "is." John F. Kennedy was simply in a rationalist Shangri-La when he told the graduates of Yale University in 1962 that the real problems of the modern world were not philosophical or ideological (and thus embroiled with issues of meaning and value) but technical and managerial. The central problem is not whether we shall apply moral norms and values to foreign policy, but how. The real issues have to do, as always, with the nature and quality of moral reasoning that is brought to bear on a particular problem. And that must be of concern to anyone with the responsibility, in public or private life, for the business of America's encounter with the world.

As to the present quality of the argument, an exceedingly mixed picture presents itself, particularly as one surveys the U.S. religious community, in which the morality and foreign policy debate is shaped to a considerable (although not exclusive) degree.

Intellectuals and activists in the great churches of mainline/oldline Protestantism—the various offshoots of Congregationalism, the Presbyterians, Methodists, and Episcopalians—seem to have reverted, in general, to a pre-Niebuhrian liberalism, now heavily influenced by the personalist psychology of Carl Rogers, feminism, and the vulgarized Marxism that informed some early expressions of liberation theology. Mainline/oldline religious leaders and activists show but the faintest traces of a Niebuhrian sense of irony and ambiguity, and indeed often seem more confident in their public policy judgments than in their theological convictions. The 1986 Methodist bishops' pastoral letter on nuclear weapons issues, "In Defense of Creation," for example, was sharply criticized by Duke Divinity School moral theologian Stanley Hauerwas as one in which "the bishops feel more comfortable condemning SDI than they do in proclaiming God's sovereignty over our existence."[6] (That Hauerwas is a principled pacifist added even more piquancy to his devastating critique of his bishops' work.) Then there is the Presbyterian Church (USA), the sponsor of a study guide that, in its original form, asked whether it was not time for American Presbyterians to think of themselves as a resistance church, on the model of the "Confessing Church" of the Barmen Declaration in Nazi Germany. Such pronouncements have raised important countercurrents; one might note the formation of such groups as Presbyterians for Democracy and Religious Freedom, in which former Undersecretary of the Navy R. James Woolsey has taken a leading role. But the mainline/oldline church bureaucracies, their principal ecumenical agencies, and the mainline/oldline Protestant peace movement remain firmly in the hands of those who would argue for some form or another of the confessing church model, set over against the principalities and powers of the contemporary American Babylon. This position seems a rather unlikely place from which to broker a wide-ranging civic conversation on morality and foreign policy.

Resurgent Protestant evangelicalism might contribute to such a conversation. In 1986, for example, the National Association of Evangelicals produced a "Guidelines" document for its new "Peace, Freedom, and Security Studies" program that challenges the mainline churches' theology and politics and calls on evangelical congregations and denominations to begin the kind of first-principles moral argument envisioned by Murray. That natural law forms of moral reasoning (even if identified by different terms, like "general revelation" or "civic righteousness") are not automatically ruled out of bounds in some evangelical circles suggests the possibility of an important new ecumenism on the morality-and-foreign-policy front.

This new ecumenism would engage, of course, Roman Catholic intellectuals, activists, and religious leaders. Here, one finds both good news and bad, from the point of view of the task identified by John Courtney Murray a generation

ago. On the asset side of the ledger, there remains significant agreement among American Catholic scholars that
mora*lism* remains an ever present danger, and that casuistry rooted in classic methods of moral reasoning is a
moral imperative. Yet there is, on the other hand, a new
Catholic moralism among activists and some bishops that
occupies a considerable position in the American Catholic
debate. Here, the traditional characteristics of *Kulturprotestantismus* – especially its fundamentalism and individualism – have been ecumenically transposed. Catholicism's
rediscovery of its scriptural heritage in the wake of the Second Vatican Council has been both a boon and a distraction
on these questions. Murray used to tell of a distinguished
journalist who was confused by the 1950s debate over morality and foreign policy because he could not understand
what foreign policy had to do with the Sermon on the
Mount; when asked by Murray why he deemed morality to
be reducible to the Sermon on the Mount, he became even
more confused and asked unhappily, "You mean it isn't?"
That question is being regularly raised by Catholic activists
(and, indeed, some bishops) today, and suggests that one
significant component of the American Catholic community will be of little help in constructing a public philosophy
able to recreate the kind of public moral argument that is
conducted without resort to biblical trump cards.

Some Jewish political intellectuals – one thinks immediately of Charles Krauthammer – are working hard at the
problem of public moral argument on foreign policy issues.[7]
Other Jewish scholars, like Rabbi David Novak of Baruch
College/CUNY in New York, are deeply interested in the
natural law tradition as it bears on issues of public policy.

Thus there is good reason to think that a new morality-
and-foreign-policy debate, exorcising Wilson's ghost and
scouting out new intellectual terrain ahead of today's right-
and left-wing moralisms, may be aborning. It will be an
interestingly diverse argument, involving as it will Roman
Catholics, evangelical Protestants, Jews, mainline Protestants who refuse to concede the field to the resistance en-

thusiasms of their brethren, and secular scholars who appreciate the imperative public need for intellectual progress beyond the rock of moralism and the hard place of relativism or realpolitik, or both.

Focusing the Debate

What would the new argument focus on? In the first instance, it would have to address, in a publicly accessible way, the question of the very meaning of "moral reasoning." Themes for such an address have been sketched above. But what about the application of moral reason to the policy agenda? Where is there room for useful debate here? Two broad areas of concern suggest themselves.

First, assuming that the United States government is not filled with pacifists or radical neo-isolationists, there is inevitably going to be a military component to America's encounter with a persistently hostile world. This suggests that the intellectual and cultural health of just war theory — that is, our ability to think through the ways in which the proportionate and discriminate use of armed force can (and cannot) contribute to peace, security, and freedom in the world — is of crucial importance.

Where is just war theory alive in American political culture? Where has it died? It is alive in our military manuals, in the Uniform Code of Military Justice, in the service academies and officer corps. It is alive among political philosophers, even if, like Stanley Hoffmann and Michael Walzer, they feel compelled to reinvent it. It is alive in international law, although usually in a truncated form. And it is alive among a goodly number of Roman Catholic, mainline and evangelical Protestant, and Jewish theologians, ethicists, and religious leaders. It is dead or dying among most religious peace activists, many religious intellectuals, and far too many ecclesiastical leaders, and among realists like Robert Tucker who continue to insist that just war theory is a matter of squaring the circle.[8]

A revival of just war theory in the argument over morality and foreign policy would address, among other things, the new pressures that modern forms of political violence – terrorism, guerrilla warfare, low-intensity conflict – have put on the classic just war criteria. International law in its present form poses one set of problems, recognizing as it does that self-defense is the only legally legitimate reason to threaten or resort to force of arms. But what constitutes self-defense in a situation of chronic ideological and political conflict such as one finds in U.S.-Soviet relations? Can just war theory adequately ground the practice of deterrence, for example, and in what form? How does one discriminate between combatants and noncombatants in guerrilla warfare? What is proportional use of force in Third World conflicts? How does one determine that the last resort has been reached, and armed force thus justified, in revolutionary situations? What does just war theory do to illuminate decisions faced by U.S. policymakers in a situation like Grenada, where the immediate threat to U.S. security is minimal but the possibilities for supporting democrats and displacing tyrants are great? And how, if at all, can just war theory's classic *ad bellum* criterion of "punishment for evil" as a legitimate moral reason for the resort to armed force help guide policy in the face of international, and particularly state-sponsored, terrorism? Absent persuasive answers to, or at least intelligent argument on, these pressing issues, the just war tradition – one important resource for considering the relationship between moral norms and foreign policy practice – may well continue to die the death of a thousand intellectual cuts in our political culture.

Such a death is also possible because just war theorists, in the main, have done a less than satisfactory job in relating their theory to the pursuit of peace. The classic forms of the just war tradition speak of the *ius ad bellum* (what William V. O'Brien has called "war-decision law") and the *ius in bello* ("war-conduct law," in O'Brien's terminology).[9] But it can also be argued – and, in an American context, must be argued – that just war theory contains, in its interstices and its basic intellectual trajectory, a *ius ad pacem*, a concept of peace as rightly ordered political community. The resort to proportionate and discriminate armed force must be directed toward peace, which is to say toward the establishment of a minimum of public order in international affairs. How this can be done in a way that avoids the sentimentalities of much contemporary "world order" thinking is a large, although not impossible, task.[10] But given the pressures placed on the classic theory by modern forms of political violence and, perhaps above all, by the fact of nuclear weapons, a just war theory that does not address the nature and pursuit of peace is unlikely to have its deservedly significant role in U.S. political discourse.

Second, the sundry theologies of liberation have contributed what seems likely to be an enduring phrase to our morality-and-foreign-policy vocabulary: there should be, they insist, a "preferential option for the poor" in devising policy affecting the world's underclass. Thanks to the work of Peter Berger, Michael Novak, and others, one can speculate and hope that the future debate on such questions of development economics will focus on means, rather than on whether such an option exists.[11]

But there is another related issue remaining to be pressed here. Should there be a "preferential option for freedom" in U.S. foreign policy? Do the world's democrats, in other words, have a special moral claim on our attention and assistance?

Experienced theorists and policymakers are dubious, indeed even skeptical, about letting the American evangelical spirit loose in the world. There are surely cautions to be observed here, as the wreckage of the presidencies of Woodrow Wilson, and more recently, Jimmy Carter, attest. But one ought to draw and maintain a clear distinction between healthy realism and cynicism. The ghost of Woodrow Wilson is not going to be exorcised by the incantations of a realpolitik that cuts straight across the grain of our national character.

Moreover, something that looks suspiciously like a democratic revolution is going on throughout the world. Fragile as the democratic achievements of recent Latin American and East Asian history may appear, they are genuine achievements. They reflect human aspirations that will not be burked. Furthermore, there are strategic reasons for supporting a "preferential option for freedom." Democratic ideology is the most persuasive answer the West can offer to the sophisticated barrage of Soviet public diplomacy in the Gorbachev era. Historically, developed democracies do not go to war with each other, and thus the democratic revolution serves the cause of peace. And, on Berger's and others' research, there would seem to be connections between democratic, or at least predemocratic, societies and economic development. Put the other way around, and as illustrated by the "four little dragons" of East Asia, economic achievement creates pressures for democratization which, if unaddressed, will eventually threaten economic achievement.

Therefore, one can make the case that a "preferential option for freedom" should occupy a central place in a post-Wilsonian consensus on morality and foreign policy. As Roman Catholic Archbishop J. Francis Stafford of Denver argued in a 1987 pastoral letter, the United States should "be a leader for ordered liberty, in and among nations."[12] The world will not become Connecticut in the twinkling of an eye, and foreign policy realists rightly warn against the perennial temptations of American universalism. But there are sufficient numbers of people in transitional Third World societies who wish, if not to be Connecticut, then at least to be ruled by something better than caudillos—peoples whose aspirations we ignore at our peril in the contest with Soviet Leninism throughout the Third World.

One can also find, in the work of dissident intellectuals such as Czechoslovakia's Vaclav Havel, Poland's Adam Michnik, and Hungary's George Konrad, claims that Western governments should support the rebuilding of a "civil society" in Soviet-dominated Central Europe.[13] Havel,

Michnik, and Konrad are not so naive as to believe that democracy is about to break out, uncontested, in Stalin's empire; but they do argue that Western support for building some measure of predemocratic institutional and cultural distance between the individual and the Leninist state serves the causes of human freedom, and, ultimately, peace. Aaron Wildavsky has made similar proposals for a U.S. policy of "containment plus pluralization" vis-à-vis the Soviet Union itself, and recent events in the USSR suggest that a conversation along these lines is not completely out of the question with Lenin's heirs.[14]

The broad and bipartisan congressional support now enjoyed by the National Endowment for Democracy (NED) suggests that the democratic revolution has, in its various forms, struck a deep chord in the American conscience. Yet there are moral quandaries here that deserve more public argument. On the one hand, how should the claims of a country's democrats be weighed against the dangers of instability in the face of an aggressive Leninist enemy which, in the case of South Korea, is as close to Seoul as Dulles Airport is to Capitol Hill? On the other hand, how do we determine when and if frustrated pressures for democratization will themselves lead to instabilities that threaten the future prospects of freedom? Then there is the question of where this dimension of the morality and foreign policy debate will be "located" in American political culture. For example, as many religious activists continue to beat a retreat from the bourgeois reformism of Corazon Aquino in the Philippines, who will make the moral case for democracy as the Philippines are caught between traditional authoritarian pressures and the New People's Army? Similar problems may be expected as mainline/oldline Protestant and ecumenical agencies turn their attention to the Korean peninsula where, depressingly if predictably, the democratic reformism of Roh Tae Woo, and the U.S. military presence in South Korea, are considered obstacles to the pursuit of peace and reunification.[15] Finally, there is the general question, by no means settled, of whether the United States has any business forcing change in other societies. By what authority do we conduct interventions for democracy around the world? A publicly persuasive answer to that question – an answer that cuts across partisan, denominational, and ideological divisions – is essential for the long-term stability of initiatives such as NED.

Beyond Circularity

Americans like problems that can be solved with some finality. We have a cultural predisposition to avoid debating such subjects as morality and foreign policy, which by nature are open-ended and perennial. But perennial need not mean "circular." It can simply mean perennial – and one can hope that such arguments will eventually lead to wisdom in policy-making as well as to shelves of scholarly books. The path beyond circularity in the American morality-and-foreign-policy debate will be open, to return to the beginning, when we recover (or in some cases, discover) that the key issue is the nature of moral reasoning itself.

Those committed to such a recovery or discovery can find inspiration (and perhaps chagrined comfort) in Jacques Maritain's description of the plight of the social ethicist. In *Man and the State* Maritain wrote:

> Moralists are unhappy people. When they insist on the immutability of moral principles, they are reproached for imposing unlivable requirements on us. When they explain the way in which those immutable principles are to be put into force, they are reproached for making morality relative. In both cases, however, they are only upholding the claims of reason to direct life.[16]

The Niebuhrian-realist rejection of moralism has been a necessary and cleansing exercise in this "nation with the soul of a church," as Gilbert Keith Chesterton once described the United States. But the realist tendency to identify morality exclusively with the moralism that characterized pre-Niebuhrian liberal Protestantism, and that characterizes post-Niebuhrian thinking on these issues in a depressingly large segment of the contemporary U.S. religious community, repeats the mistake it attempts to correct. There is another way to go at this, and that is to rediscover the tradition of moral reasoning as exemplified (but hardly exhausted) by the natural law tradition of Murray and Maritain. If, with Maritain, we believe that reason rather than unbridled passion ought to direct life (and even public policy), there is considerable work to be done in reconstructing the way in which we conduct public moral argument over America's right role in world affairs.

2

A Question of Honor—The War
Novels of Evelyn Waugh

What with the successful television production of
Brideshead Revisited, a critically acclaimed movie version
of *A Handful of Dust*, and the publication of the first volume of Martin Stannard's massive biography, an Evelyn
Waugh revival seems well under way.[1] Indeed Edmund
Morris, reviewing Stannard's work for the *New York Times
Book Review*, argued that "the title 'master,' applied in this
century only to Henry James and (reverently by Evelyn
Waugh) to P. G. Wodehouse, is beginning to glow like a nim-
bus about the head of Waugh himself."[2] No doubt Waugh
would be vastly amused by some of the absurdities that at-
tend modern literary canonization—for example, the idea
that squadrons of graduate students are now sweating over
dissertations with such titles as "The Influence of Spengler
on Evelyn Waugh's Critique of the Civilization of the Flap-
per Era," or somesuch. But Waugh's posthumous (and over-
due) recognition as a "master" of English prose affords other, and one hopes, more serious opportunities to consider
not only his literary style, but his contributions to our understanding of modernity and its discontents. And among
the latter, one should not neglect Waugh's insights into the
tangled question of morality and international affairs.
  Of course, putting the matter as baldly as that risks

the kind of mockery that rightfully attends the making of some dissertations, for Waugh could hardly claim to be a specialist in theology, moral philosophy, or international relations. Waugh was a novelist and critic, and it is as such that his work should be primarily judged. Yet those who wish to think through issues at the intersection of moral norms and international politics could do far worse than to reflect on Waugh's trilogy of novels about World War II—books that may yet be recognized as Waugh's masterwork.

The novels in question—*Men at Arms, Officers and Gentlemen*, and *Unconditional Surrender* (*The End of the Battle*, in the unhappily renamed U.S. edition)—were written over a ten-year span, between 1951 and 1961, and were subsequently reedited by the author into a single volume entitled *Sword of Honor*.[3] In the trilogy, which Waugh intended as a single reflection on "the crisis of civilization which reached its climax in World War II,"[4] Waugh drew extensively on his own considerable experiences in the war, which ranged from raids on West Africa through the battle of Crete and on to his membership with Randolph Churchill in the British mission to Tito's partisans in Yugoslavia.

Those experiences are fictionally recreated in the adventures and misadventures of the trilogy's protagonist, Guy Crouchback, the sole surviving son of an old English Catholic family. As *Men at Arms* opens, Guy, who has suffered throughout the 1930s from an ignominious divorce and an altogether useless and boring life, returns to England from self-exile in Italy to volunteer for the armed services. But the thirty-six-year-old Guy is motivated by more than simple patriotic duty; he sees the war in dramatic, indeed primarily moral, terms. The news of the Ribbentrop-Molotov pact (which made temporary allies of Hitler and Stalin while ensuring the liquidation of Poland) rouses Guy to action from his spiritual torpor:

> News that shook the politicians and young poets of a dozen capital cities brought deep peace to one English heart. . . . [Guy had] expected his country to go to war

in a panic, for all the wrong reasons or for no reason at all, with the wrong allies, in pitiful weakness. But now, splendidly, everything had become clear. The enemy at last was plain in view, huge and hateful, all disguise cast off. It was the Modern Age in arms. Whatever the outcome there was a place for him in that battle.[5]

Guy quickly learns, in his London club, that his crusading views are not widely shared. His smugly self-satisfied brother-in-law, Arthur Box-Bender, a Tory backbencher, tries to put Guy to rights:

> "I'm afraid you won't get much encouragement. All that sort of thing happened in 1914 — retired colonels dyeing their hair and enlisting in the ranks. . . . All very gallant of course but it won't happen this time. The whole thing is planned. The Government knows just how many men they can handle; they know where they can get them; they'll take them in their own time."[6]

Undeterred, Guy eventually joins the Royal Corps of Halberdiers as a junior officer in training. The Halberdiers are an ancient regiment whose traditions seem to fit Guy's romantic conception of the soldierly life. But Guy is soon caught up in the bureaucratic maelstrom of total war, and a series of aimless training exercises whittle down his enthusiasm to the point where he begins to entertain "the sickening suspicion . . . that he was engaged in a war in which courage and a just cause were quite irrelevant to the issue."[7]

Nor does Guy find many of his fellow officers thinking of the war in terms of a moral crusade with world-historical consequences. Even Colonel Tommy Blackhouse, the Coldstreamer in whom Waugh comes closest to a sympathetic portrait of the thoroughly modern "officer and gentleman," is of the opinion that "it's going to be a long war. The great thing is to spend it among friends."[8] Nor, when the Soviet Union invaded Poland, did Guy find much sympathy for his own high dudgeon:

"My dear fellow, we've got quite enough on our hands as it is. We can't go to war with the whole world."

"Then why go to war at all? If all we want is prosperity, the hardest bargain Hitler made would be preferable to victory. If we are concerned with justice the Russians are as guilty as the Germans."

"Justice?" said the old soldiers. "Justice?"

"Besides," said Box-Bender when Guy spoke to him of the matter that seemed in no one's mind but his, "the country would never stand for it. The socialists have been crying blue murder against the Nazis for five years but they are all pacifists at heart. So far as they have any feeling of patriotism it's for Russia. You'd have a general strike and the whole country in collapse if you set up to be just."

"Then what are we fighting for?"

"Oh, we had to do that, you know. . . . If we sat tight now there'd be chaos. What we have to do now is to limit and localize the war, not extend it."[9]

Yet Guy soldiers on, in company with one of Waugh's greatest comic creations, a magnificently drawn fraud named Apthorpe, and under the leadership of General Ben Ritchie-Hook, an English condottiere who hasn't been socialized into the modern etiquette of war, and whose single-minded approach to strategy and tactics involves "biffing" the enemy at every opportunity.

Ritchie-Hook's "biffing" eventually lands Guy in trouble during a raid on Dakar, after which Guy, whom others wrongly suppose to have "blotted his copybook" during the action, is temporarily seconded to Blackhouse's Commando unit, which is training in Scotland under the occasionally watchful eye of Hazardous Offensive Operations headquarters (HOO HQ): "that bizarre product of total war which later was to proliferate through five acres of valuable London property, engrossing the simple high staff officers of all the Services with experts, charlatans, plain lunatics, and every unemployed member of the British Communist Party."[10]

His service in the Commando unit takes Guy to Alexandria, "ancient asparagus bed of theological absurdity,"[11] where his confession is heard by a priest who turns out to be a German agent, and eventually to Crete, just as the British forces are being routed from the island. In the endgame of that debacle, his closest friend in the Commando, Ivor Claire, whom Guy had thought of as "the fine flower of them all . . . quintessential England, the man Hitler had not taken into account,"[12] disobeys the surrender order and deserts his troops. But Guy manages to escape capture and, after a harrowing crossing of the Mediterranean in an open boat, lands back in Alexandria where he convalesces and wonders, again, precisely what it is he is fighting for:

> It was just such a sunny, breezy Mediterranean day two years before when he read of the Russo-German alliance, when a decade of shame seemed to be ending in light and reason, when the Enemy was plainly in view, huge and hateful, all disguise cast off; the modern age in arms. Now that hallucination was dissolved, like the whales and turtles on the voyage from Crete, and he was back after less than two years' pilgrimage in a Holy Land of illusion in the old ambiguous world, where priests were spies and gallant friends proved traitors and his country was led blundering into dishonour.[13]

Officers and Gentlemen ends at this point in the saga, and it would be another six years before Waugh, who had erroneously thought himself creatively burned out on the subject, resumed his story with *Unconditional Surrender*. It is now 1944. Guy has spent the intervening two years back with the Halberdiers, on various training exercises.

Then, through the machinations of another of Waugh's absurdist characters, the Corporal of Horse become literary modernist named Ludovic, Guy is assigned as a liaison officer to the "Headquarters of the British Mission to the Anti-Fascist Forces of National Liberation (Adriatic)." Beneath the euphemism there are, of course, the Communist partisan forces of Tito, who are occasionally battling the Germans and constantly fighting the Yugoslav royalists loyal to the government-in-exile in London. Guy, who has decided that if national honor is impossible, personal honor may yet be preserved, takes up the cause of a ragged band of Jewish refugees who, having escaped from the Nazis, are now at the mercy of the anti-Semitic Communist partisans. But even here his efforts at decency amidst total war partially backfire, for although he arranges for the repatriation of most of the refugees, his friendliness toward their spokesmen, a couple named Kanyi, results in the latters' liquidation by the partisans with the connivance of Communist sympathizers among the British mission. Madame Kanyi's last conversation with Guy forces home the question that has been harrowing Waugh's protagonist throughout the trilogy:

> "Is there any place that is free of evil? It is too simple to say that only the Nazis wanted war. These communists wanted it too. It was the only way in which they could come to power. Many of my people wanted it, to be revenged on the Germans, to hasten the creation of the national state. It seems to me there was a will to war, a death wish, everywhere. Even good men thought their private honor would be satisfied by war. They could assert their manhood by killing and being killed. They would accept hardships in recompense for having been selfish and lazy. Danger justified privilege. I knew Italians—not very many perhaps—who felt this. Were there none in England?"

> "God forgive me," said Guy, "I was one of them."[14]

The Procrustean Bed of Bureaucracy

"God is in the details," Albert Einstein used to insist, and the same might be said of literary genius. At one (not inconsequential) level, Evelyn Waugh's trilogy is a brilliant, telling, and minutely drawn satire of bureaucratic life, and a profound, if occasionally bitter, reflection on how the bureaucratization of the modern military tends to erode the classic mores of the soldier's craft.[15]

All wars are conducted in the fog of battle rather than with the clarity of vision that historical hindsight provides. But modern warfare has vastly extended the confusion, in Waugh's view. The participant in modern war, Waugh seems to argue, is akin to a man looking through the wrong end of a telescope. The modern soldier finds himself viewing everything in microcosm, and the larger issues of the conflict become blurred perhaps beyond recognition.[16] During the fall of France in 1940, for example, Guy's regiment is absurdly shuffled back and forth:

> For those who followed events and thought about the future, the world's foundations seemed to shake. For the Halberdiers it was one damned thing after another. . . . Chaos in Liverpool. Quays and ships in absolute darkness. Bombs falling somewhere not far distant. Embarkation staff officers scanning nominal-rolls with dimmed torches. Guy and his company were ordered into one ship, ordered out again, stood-to on the dockside for an hour.[17]

Where, amidst all this vast confusion, is one to discern the cause for which one serves? How, in other words and in the language of the classical moral tradition, is the *ius ad bellum* to be discovered?

Modernity's confusions, which for Waugh involved a profound tension between the civilized individual and the barbarian crowd, are rarely far removed from farce in Waugh's work, and the war trilogy is no exception to this pattern. The bureaucratic inversions of modern war, Waugh seems to imply, are just too much for ordinary minds to come to grips with. As, for example, in this memorable scene involving Guy Crouchback's transfer to the Commandos:

> "Sergeant-Major, we have Mr. Crouchback's leave address?"
>
> "Marine Hotel, Matchet, sir."
>
> "Then make out a move order for him to report forthwith to HOO HQ."
>
> "Am I to give the address, sir?"
>
> "That wouldn't do. It's on the Most Secret List."
>
> "Sir."
>
> Ten minutes later, the Adjutant remarked: "Sergeant-Major, if we withhold the address, how will Mr. Crouchback know where to report?"
>
> "Sir."
>
> "We could refer it back to HOO HQ."
>
> "Sir."
>
> "But it is marked 'Immediate Action.'"
>
> "Sir."
>
> These two men of no consequence at all sat silent and despairing.[18]

But the chaos of large organizations caught in the grindings of history is more than a matter for satire and ridicule. The bureaucratization of "total war," Waugh suggests, further diminishes modern man's already depleted reserves of initiative and moral responsibility. This theme is incarnated in the pathetic figure of Major "Fido" Hound, whom one critic has described as "the epitome of all the most savage views of the regimental officers on 'the staff.'"[19] As a senior staff officer, Fido holds a large responsibility for others' lives. But his own human weaknesses, magnified rather than compensated for by the iron cage of bureaucracy, render him manifestly incapable of making sense, much less moral judgments. Trying to put his uncomprehending superiors "in the picture" during the Cretan debacle, Fido can only bring himself to go through the bureaucratic motions laid down in a nearly forgotten bedlam of training manuals: "For Major Hound, it was enough that the words should be spoken, the correct sounds made even into the void of their utter weariness."[20] Later in the rout, when Fido is blindly scrambling about for food, his sole comfort is that he holds a requisition order from higher authorities: "He did not, even in his extremity, quite abandon his faith in the magic of official forms. In bumf lay salvation."[21] Bureaucracy, Waugh implies, has become not only the substitute for authority; it has eroded the moral possibilities of soldierly leadership for all but premodern relics like Brigadier Ritchie-Hook who insist on defying the current conventions and bureaucratic mores.

Waugh was not the first author, of course, to note that the modern "nation at arms" gave enormous scope for all manner of frauds, incompetents, cranks, and self-seekers. But few novelists have so ably and acidly sketched the myriad ways in which the sheer size of modern political-military organizations affords unprecedented opportunities for mischief. Waugh's organizational whipping boy in this regard is the aforementioned "Hazardous Offensive Operations" unit (loosely modeled on the Combined Operations department of Lord Louis Mountbatten), which by 1943 had metastasized into "numerous mansions from Hendon to Clapham in which small bands of experts in untroubled privacy made researches into fortifying drugs, invisible maps, noiseless explosives, and other projects dear to the heart of the healthy schoolboy. There was even a Swahili witch doctor in rooms off the Edgware Road who had been engaged to cast spells on the Nazi leaders."

The latter, Dr. Akonanga, an abortionist in prior life, figures prominently in one of the trilogy's most bizarre scenes. Virginia, Guy Crouchback's former wife, is desperately searching for a doctor who will abort her pregnancy, itself the result of a public relations scam engineered by the vilely ambitious Lord Kilbannock (one of several fictional characters through whom Waugh tormented Brendan Bracken). Kilbannock's housemaid recommends Dr. Akonanga, but on entering his offices, Virginia discovers that the doctor has other things on his mind:

> She stepped into a room whose conventional furniture was augmented with a number of handdrums, a bright statue of the Sacred Heart, a cock, decapitated but unplucked, secured with nails to the table top, its wings spread open like a butterfly's, a variety of human bones including a skull, a brass cobra of Benares ware, bowls of ashes, flasks from a chemical laboratory stoppered and holding murky liquids. A magnified photograph of Mr. Winston Churchill glowered down upon the profusion of Dr. Akonanga's war-stores. . . .
>
> "Dr. Akonanga," [Virginia] asked, "what can you think you are doing that is more important than me?"
>
> "I am giving Herr Ribbentrop the most terrible dreams," said Dr. Akonanga with pride and gravity.[22]

Then there are the conspiracy theorists in HOO's security section, led by Colonel Grace-Groundling-Marchpole, whose

> department was so secret that it communicated only with the War Cabinet and Chiefs of Staff. Colonel Marchpole kept his information until it was asked for. To date that had not occurred and he rejoiced under neglect. Premature examination of his files might ruin his private, undefined Plan. Somewhere in the ultimate curlicues of his mind, there was a Plan. Given time, given enough confidential material, he would succeed in knitting the entire quarrelsome world into a single net of conspiracy in which there were no antagonists, merely millions of men working, unknown to one another, for the same end; and there would be no more war.[23]

Bureaucratization leads to more than the mischief of frauds and charlatans, however; in Waugh's fictional world it also magnifies evils that an older society kept at bay through the traditional institutions of family, church, and class. Lord Kilbannock himself is a prime example of this. A minor Scottish peer, and a former horseracing correspondent of limited talent, Ian Kilbannock confesses to having become "pretty red" during the Spanish civil war, but not quite red enough to cut down on his time at Bellamy's Club, an elite bastion of the London male social scene. Still, Ian knows where the deals have to be cut, with whom, and how, to secure his postwar comfort. Transposing himself from journalist to press agent (a move that H. L. Mencken used to describe as the quintessence of personal corruption), Kilbannock proceeds to manipulate the mass public for subsequent personal gain. "This is a People's War," proclaims this peer of the realm, "and the People won't have poetry and they won't have flowers. Flowers stink. The upper classes are on the secret list. We want heroes of the people, to and for the people, by, with, and from the people."[24] To which end Kilbannock creates, whole cloth, the "people's hero," Major Trimmer, who in prior life was the women's hairdresser on the *Aquitania*. Guy Crouchback's occasional acts of modest heroism go unnoticed, or enter the bureaucratic ledgers as blots on his "copybook." Trimmer, who walked through life "with all the panache of a mongrel among the dustbins, tail waving, ears cocked, nose a-quiver,"[25] a coward and fraud who has done literally nothing of consequence for the war effort, is transmuted by modern press agentry into a figure in the mold of Nelson and Wellington, and makes Kilbannock's career as a publicist to be reckoned with.

It is a staple of Waugh criticism to argue that the novelist was obsessed with a search for order amidst the chaos of modernity, and many commentators have seen Waugh's intellectual conversion to Catholicism as an attempt to link the search for wholeness with the quest for holiness.[26] There is much to be said in defense of that analysis, but it should not be taken to mean that Waugh thought of modern politics as so irredeemably corrupt that good men must necessarily retreat into sectarian marginality. Perhaps despite itself, modernity presented men with causes worth fighting for, and if Waugh's Catholicism included a romantic element it was also deeply imbued with what a theological historian might term Christian realism.[27] As Madame Kanyi, the doomed representative of the Jewish refugees, understood, no place is entirely free from evil, and those who pretend otherwise often end up as instruments of the very evil they wish to combat.

The issue of the age thus cannot be understood as the Quixotic quest for a moral Archimedean point from which one can create a perfect world. The choices men faced at the intersection of ethics and politics were often between bad and worse; that was, or ought to be, a given. The important point, for both individuals and societies, was not to lose sight of the transcendent horizon that gave content to such often flaccid words as "good" and "evil." Men of honor, and governments, could resist the moral Procrustean bed of political-military bureaucracy; there was room, even amidst the iron cage, for moral initiative and responsible decision making. No doubt, for Waugh, that task of creating a moral identity, in either personal or societal terms, had been rendered immeasurably more difficult by modernity. But carving out space for the exercise of conscience was difficult, though not impossible—if one could somehow see beyond the microcosm to the larger issues engaged by the war.

This was not, however, a moral skill that had been well developed by the Allied leadership, in Waugh's view.

The Compromise with Totalitarianism

The central moral image of Waugh's war trilogy is a sword, found in the church of St. Dulcina, near the Castello Crouchback where Guy has spent his prewar Italian exile. The sword is a relic of Roger of Waybroke, a medieval English knight:

Roger's manor had long ago been lost and overbuilt. He
left it for the second Crusade, sailed from Genoa, and
was shipwrecked on this coast. There he enlisted under
the local Count, who promised to take him to the Holy
Land but led him first against a neighbor, on the walls
of whose castle he fell at the moment of victory. The
count gave him honourable burial and there he had lain
through the centuries, while the church crumbled and
was rebuilt above him, far from Jerusalem, far from
Waybroke, a man with a great journey still all before
him and a great vow unfulfilled; but the people of Santa
Dulcina delle Rocce, to whom the supernatural order in
all its ramifications was ever present and ever more
lively than the humdrum world about them, adopted
Sir Roger and despite all clerical remonstrance
canonized him, brought him their troubles and touched
his sword for luck, so that its edge was always bright.
All his life, but especially in recent years, Guy had felt
an especial kinship with "il Santo Inglese." Now, on his
last day, he made straight for the tomb and ran his
finger, as the fisherman did, along the knight's sword.
"Sir Roger, pray for me," he said, "and for our endan-
gered kingdom."[28]

Thus the opening scene of *Men at Arms*. Two volumes
later, *Unconditional Surrender* begins with what Waugh evidently intended as a demonic mirror image, also of a sword,
in this case the brilliantly tempered and bejeweled "Sword
of Stalingrad," which King George VI had commissioned as
a gift to the Soviet people, in the person of Josef Stalin, in
homage to the breaking of the siege of Stalingrad. And in
this gift, and the circumstances in which it was publicly
displayed at Westminster Abbey, Waugh saw the dishonor
into which, he judged, his country had been led:

The sword . . . stood upright between two candles, on a
table counterfeiting an altar. . . . It had been made at
King's command as a gift to "the steel-hearted people of
Stalingrad." An octogenarian, who had made ceremoni-
al swords for five sovereigns, rose from his bed to forge

it; silver, gold, rock-crystal, and enamel had gone to its embellishment. . . . The gossip writer for the *Daily Express* suggested it should be sent around the kingdom. Cardiff, Birmingham, Sheffield, Manchester, Glasgow, and Edinburgh paid it secular honours in their Art Galleries and Guild Halls. Now, back from its tour, it reached its apotheosis, exposed for adoration hard by the shrine of St. Edward the Confessor and the sacring place of the kings of England.[29]

Evelyn Waugh's contempt for the Grand Alliance, which his friend and biographer Christopher Sykes dismissed as a reflection of the novelist's "naive and impractical political ideas,"[30] is, obviously, a debatable point in considering the history of the twentieth century in general and World War II in particular. But Christopher Sykes is surely wrong to disparage Waugh's profound sense of the myriad ways, large and small, in which modern totalitarian politics had put great pressure, perhaps even to the breaking point, on the classic Western moral understanding of the just war and its relationship to the pursuit of peace, freedom, and justice, for both individuals and nations. In truth, one could argue that Waugh's trilogy stands with such classics as Arthur Koestler's *Darkness at Noon*, Ignazio Silone's *Bread and Wine*, and André Malraux's *Man's Fate* as a literary reflection on the moral meaning of the totalitarian project in history. Koestler, Silone, and Malraux were principally focused on the impact of Marxist totalitarianism—"the God that failed," in Richard Crossman's famous image—on individual moral choice. But Waugh, who was hardly insensitive to this dimension of totalitarianism (emblematically represented in Guy Crouchback's tragic relationship to the Kanyis), extended the discussion by asking whether the very nature of totalitarian politics—the assertion of a consciously antitranscendent amorality masking as the true humanism—rendered the classic Christian moral theory of statecraft moot. In a modern age scarred by the impact of totalitarian politics—in this "war of attrition which raged ceaselessly against the human spirit"—could there be honor for nations, or only for individuals?[31]

Waugh may seem, at first blush, to suggest the latter. Against the single-minded devotion to the Communist cause embodied in characters such as the homosexual diplomat Sir Ralph Brompton, the Oxford logical positivist Joe Cattermole, and fellow Halberdier officer Frank DeSouza, Guy Crouchback is singularly ineffectual.[32] He is, as Waugh once described him to his friend Anthony Powell, "a prig [but a] virtuous, brave prig."[33] But Guy at least tries, and he recognizes the dilemmas into which his encounter with the totalitarian project has thrust him. Others, Waugh suggests, are far more culpable before the bar of history—the Labor politicians whose real patriotism is ideological; the Tory politicians and the London elites whose primary concern is maintaining their privileged position in society; Winston Churchill, with his hubris about being able to manage "Uncle Joe" and his parceling out of spheres of influence in postwar Europe; the left-leaning, fellow-traveling, or outright Communist intellectuals, whom Waugh seems to find even more appalling than Tito's partisans, for to the latter's simple brutality the dons add a cynicism masquerading as a higher morality.

Waugh's summary judgment on the social, intellectual, and political leadership of Britain in the face of totalitarianism is unremittingly harsh: those who did not understand that Hitler and Stalin were two sides of the same diabolical coin had misread the central moral question of modern world politics. And thus a sword forged by royal fiat as a gift to a mass murderer comes to be venerated "hard by the shrine of St. Edward the Confessor and the sacring place of the kings of England."

The image is an extraordinarily powerful one, but it should not be thought that Waugh had fallen into a kind of bitter despair over the future of civilization, which he identified with the fate of the West. In 1949, writing to George Orwell to thank him for a gift copy of 1984, Waugh summa-

rized his views on what it would take to confront successful-
ly the totalitarian project:

> I have seen a number of reviews, English & American,
> all respectful and appreciative. I won't repeat what
> they say. Please believe that I echo their admiration for
> your ingenuity. . . .
>
> But the book failed to make my flesh creep as pre-
> sumably you intended. For one thing I think your
> metaphysics are wrong. You deny the soul's existence
> (at least Winston [Smith, the protagonist of *1984*] does)
> and can only contrast matter with reason & will. It is
> now apparent that matter can control reason and will in
> certain conditions. So you are left with nothing but
> matter. . . .
>
> Winston's rebellion was false. His "Brotherhood"
> (whether real or imaginary) was simply another gang
> like the Party. And it was false, to me, that the form of
> his revolt should simply be fucking in the style of Lady
> Chatterley—finding reality through a sort of mystical
> union with the Proles in the sexual act. I think it possi-
> ble that in 1984 we shall be living in conditions rather
> like those you show. But what makes your version spu-
> rious to me is the disappearance of the Church. . . . Dis-
> regard all the supernatural implications if you like, but
> you must admit its unique character as a social & his-
> torical institution. I believe it is inextinguishable,
> though of course it can be extinguished in a certain
> place for a certain time. . . .
>
> The Brotherhood which can confound the Party is
> one of love, not adultery, still less throwing vitriol in
> children's faces. And men who have loved a crucified
> God need never think of torture as all-powerful.[34]

Unless one argues that the Waugh who wrote this powerful letter in 1949 had radically changed his views between
then and 1961, when *Unconditional Surrender* was published, one cannot argue that Waugh saw no possibility for
honorable national action in international politics. But the
condition for the possibility of a morally sound politics in

the age of totalitarianism had to be conversion – in Waugh's robust (and, by his own description, "sectarian") Catholic view, a reconversion of Western culture to its deepest religious roots. The totalitarians understood what the decent but blind West did not – that politics was an expression of culture and that the heart of culture was religion or, to borrow from Paul Tillich, the incarnation of an "ultimate concern." The totalitarian challenge, which was metaphysical and moral even before it was political and military, had to be engaged at that fundamental level. Unless the West could reconstruct a sense of what it stood for, it would prove impossible to resist what it claimed to be against.

Christopher Sykes suggests, with reason, that "when the war was over Evelyn was a bitter, disillusioned, angry man. He was horrified to think that we had defeated Nazi Germany only in alliance with Soviet Russia and with Hitler's equal in crime, Stalin. He was on bad terms with his times."[35] One could argue, of course, that ours are times with which it is a good thing to be on bad terms. But it seems truer to say that Waugh, for all his crankiness and romanticism, had seen through the fog of war to the heart of the essential struggle in modern world politics more clearly than those Englishmen who, even today, insist on referring to the Soviet Union as "Russia," as if the modern Soviet state were simply the Czar's kingdom in different dress.

The Choice for Honor

It is one thing, of course, to argue that Waugh had a finely tuned sense of modern ideological politics, and another to suggest that he defined a workable and morally satisfactory solution to the dilemmas of statecraft in the world of the late twentieth century. No claims on behalf of Waugh's omniscience on this latter score ought to be made. In fact, there is quite probably a contradiction, or perhaps better, a dead end, in Waugh's thought here.

His claim that a West capable of confronting the totalitarian project would have to be a West that had recovered a sense of its moral roots in that culture formed in the interaction of Jerusalem and Athens may be (in fact, I think it is) sound. But Waugh seemed to suggest that such a recovery would take place only in a reconstituted Christendom, indeed a reconstituted Pax Romana, in the literal sense of that term. This may have been, to some extent, the vision of Pope Pius XII, whom Waugh greatly admired. But it has not been the view of Pius's successors. Moreover, Waugh's palpable disaffection for democracy, the contemporary political bearer of the classic Western tradition of political morality, ill fits contemporary Catholic social theory. In the person of Pope John Paul II, this theory teaches that democracy is the form of governance which, under modern conditions, best incarnates those moral norms that Waugh believed essential to humane social life, a life capable of honor.[36] And by "democracy," contemporary Catholic social thought does not mean Christendom, but a democratic pluralism informed and sustained by moral norms derived from the classic heritage of the West. With all respect, it cannot be said that this is a view with which Evelyn Waugh greatly sympathized.

In sum, then, Waugh's war trilogy is best understood, not as a full-blown literary prescription for thinking through the dilemmas of morality and foreign policy, but as a brilliantly achieved cautionary tale. Evelyn Waugh was enough of a historian to know that one runs risks by thinking of one's own times as utterly without precedent; one can imagine Waugh's derisory response to Father Theodore Hesburgh's claim that today's bishops, confronting the perils of world politics in the nuclear age, find themselves in a situation in which "there [are] no precedents to invoke, no history to depend upon for a wise lesson, no real body of theology except for that which dates back to pacifism or a just-war doctrine that was first applied in the days of spears, swords, bows and arrows, not ICBMs."[37] But Waugh's Christian realism, combined with his penetrating insight into the human yearnings on which the totalitarian project fed, led him to an understanding of what was distinctive about his times that statesmen and moral theorists will ignore at their intellectual and political peril. In this sense, Waugh's abiding concern for "honor" should not be regarded as a form of premodern, medieval romanticism, but as an attempt to define one crucial meaning of "moral action" in contemporary political and military life.

We, too, have to choose, if metaphorically, between the sword of Roger of Waybroke and the Sword of Stalingrad: between a politics that holds itself accountable to moral norms that transcend it and a politics in which the will-to-power is the sole guiding principle. That choice is not the only choice we must make. But it is the choice that gives substantive definition to all those secondary choices between relative goods and evils that constitute the bulk of political life. Understanding that is one indispensable part of the recovery of honor, the recovery of moral discourse about international politics in the late twentieth century.

3

Nuclear Deterrence and the
Common Morality

Arguments over nuclear weapons and strategy often use the conceit of a "scenario" – an imaginary sequence of events – to test hypotheses, weigh the implications of alternative policies, and draw prescriptive conclusions. The same intellectual tactic may be used in testing the moral argument over nuclear deterrence. Consider, in that regard, this scenario:

In the midst of a decade that has witnessed the formal (and generally left-of-center) leadership of mainline Protestantism and Roman Catholicism express the gravest reservations about the morality of deterrence, a new book enters the lists. Its authors are Catholic scholars specializing in constitutional law, philosophical ethics, and theological ethics. Each of the authors is a principled anti-Communist; each regards the Western democratic project as morally superior to Soviet totalitarianism. Moreover, the authors recognize that deterrence has "worked" – that it has been instrumental in preventing World War III.

The authors are committed to a form of moral reasoning that they style "common morality," which is to say, "natural law morality." In that great tradition as they understand it, it is absolutely forbidden to kill innocents. That is what abortion does. That is what murderers do. And that, they argue, is what deterrence intends. The logic of deterrence, they argue, inevitably involves the threat to kill innocents, through "city-swaps" or "final retaliation" nuclear attack. And so, even if the buttons are never pushed, the deterrence system is immoral, because it necessarily involves a conditional intention to commit murder.

Because the deterrence system is inherently immoral, they conclude, it should be rejected outright. The authors concede that this will have undesirable consequences. At best, the abandonment of deterrence will involve the Finlandization of the West. At worst, it might lead to direct Soviet control of the democracies. The authors are quite clear that these likely outcomes are not moral goods. Many people may be killed or enslaved. But a calculus that gives significant weight to consequences makes no difference in the "common morality," as they conceive it. In a morality abstracted from consequences, deterrence is immoral, and deterrence should be rejected. Until then, those involved in the deterrence system are objectively involved in a moral atrocity or, as the catechism once put it, in mortal sin.

Such an argument, one might well imagine, would enliven the continuing debate about the morality of deterrence, because the authors' understanding of who was "wrong" on this question would be breathtakingly comprehensive, running the spectrum from Pope John Paul II through the French, German, and American bishops and their advisers, to "minimal" deterrers in the policy community such as Robert McNamara and Gerard Smith. At the popular level the debate would be equally bracing, unilateral disarmament and anticommunism usually being found on the opposite ends of the polemical barricades. Anti-Communists, and especially those who shared the authors' commitment to natural law forms of moral reasoning, would be, variously, puzzled, aggravated, and/or distressed. Nuclear unilateralists, including many who would reject the authors' moral methodology and conclusions as applied to virtually every other hotly contested public policy issue (for example, abortion), would be ecstatic: here, at long last, was a "conservative" defense of unilateralism, one that could perhaps persuade the Vatican to condemn deterrence. Such a book, were it written, would be "in play" for years to come.

Thus the scenario. But there is one caveat: this is not an exercise in fantasy or imagination. The book has been written. John Finnis, Joseph Boyle, and Germain Grisez have written it.[1] *Nuclear Deterrence, Morality and Realism* is very much "in play." But how? And to what ends?

Beyond the Bernardin Barrier

According to the semiofficial history of the deliberations leading to the 1983 pastoral letter of the U.S. Catholic bishops, "The Challenge of Peace," Archbishop Joseph Bernardin, the drafting committee chairman, began the committee's work in 1982 by stating that the committee's one ground rule was that "it would not, under any circumstances, support unilateral nuclear disarmament."[2] Long before the Finnis-Boyle-Grisez volume, one wondered, why? If the bishops were actually conducting a principled moral analysis, then surely no possible prudential outcomes could be preemptively excluded. If, on the other hand, the bishops' primary audience was the policy community, wherein unilateral disarmament is considered a species of mental illness, the Bernardin prohibition makes pragmatic, if not precisely theological, sense.[3]

That the Catholic debate over nuclear weapons and strategy in the 1980s has been excessively beholden to political calculations is also suggested by the voting that took place on the final draft of "The Challenge of Peace" in May 1983. Unilateralist and pacifist bishops such as Thomas Gumbleton of Detroit, Raymond Hunthausen of Seattle, and Leroy Matthiesen of Amarillo voted in favor of a document that flatly contradicted some of their most cherished moral claims (for example, that unilateral disarmament was a moral imperative and that pacifism could form the basis of foreign and defense policy).[4] Conversely, classic just war bishops such as Philip Hannan of New Orleans and Austin Vaughan of New York voted their moral and political convictions by numbering themselves among the eight lonely opponents of the final draft.

Now one can argue, and in Catholic terms one ought to argue, that the Holy Spirit can work through horsetrading as well as through direct illumination of the soul. The horsetrading that preceded final passage of "The Challenge of Peace" was not, in and of itself, offensive. In many respects it contributed to a wiser final document. But the fact remains that there was an intellectual untidiness about "The Challenge of Peace" from the beginning. Moreover, one ought not expect too much by way of relief pitching, even from the Holy Spirit. "The Challenge of Peace" was a compromise statement, and many of the compromises within it were directly attributable to the bishops' desire to be "players" (in that worst of Beltway vulgarisms) in the policy debate at its narrowest end. The tensions in the pastoral letter's moral analysis and prudential prescriptions reflect that fact. And thus it was entirely predictable that "The Challenge of Peace" confused aspects of the moral debate over deterrence as well as offering needed clarifications.

That debate has been further complicated by the events of the past six years. President Reagan's Strategic Defense Initiative has shaken the foundations of the strategic debate as they had not been shaken since the 1950s; not the least reason for that was the way in which the president himself seemed to question the moral legitimacy of deterrence. The Intermediate Nuclear Force treaty challenged the assumption, shared broadly within the religious community and explicitly by "The Challenge of Peace," that nuclear force modernizations could rarely, if ever, contribute to the reduction or elimination of nuclear weapons. The INF treaty has also reopened a vigorous debate over the possible linkage between strategic nuclear force reductions and conventional arms, as well as sharpening the debate over force modernization and its relationship to strategic stability, "deep cuts" in strategic weaponry, and the emerging capabilities of strategic defense. Those who wish to enter the thicket of argument over the morality of deterrence thus find themselves in an exponentially complexified strategic, technological, political, and, indeed, ethical situation.

Concurrently, the actions of several other church bodies following the appearance of "The Challenge of Peace" have demonstrated that the question of a wise and publicly accepted moral framework for arguing these questions is anything but settled. The bishops of the United Methodist Church tried to "go beyond" the Catholic bishops by declaring deterrence idolatrous. Still, they claimed that this did not require immediate unilateral disarmament – for, one assumes, the same pragmatic reasons that may have been part of Archbishop Bernardin's calculations in 1982.[5] The Presbyterian Church (USA) issued a study guide on "peacemaking" that asked whether, given the nuclear reality and on the model of the Confessing Church in Nazi Germany, U.S. Presbyterians were not now "called to resistance." Responding to pressures from the pacifist-unilateralist wing of the U.S. episcopate, the U.S. Catholic bishops issued a kind of moral report card on the strategic situation five years after "The Challenge of Peace," a report that expressed grave skepticism about strategic defense while moving the bishops even further down the path toward a "minimum deterrence" posture.[6] Parallel to this debate, pressures have been exerted on Pope John Paul II to release a study by the Pontifical Academy of Sciences that virtually condemns strategic defense in general, and the Reagan administration's SDI program in particular.

Given this rich (some would say, far too rich) menu of ecclesiastical judgments on various aspects of deterrence and nuclear strategy at the policy level, one comes to a book like *Nuclear Deterrence, Morality and Realism* with a profound sense of relief, because the highest compliment that can be paid the Finnis-Boyle-Grisez volume is that it reorients the discussion to questions of first principles in moral reasoning. Moreover, and unlike the Methodist bishops' letter and the Presbyterian study guide, the authors resolutely reject the psychologization of politics and strategy. They are under no illusions about communism. They do not believe that U.S.-Soviet conflict is caused by misunderstanding, bad communications, and the rest of the Rogerian catalogue of sins, offenses, and negligences. *Nuclear Deterrence, Morality and Realism* is rooted in the classic understanding that politics is the business of men, not angels; that, like all human enterprises, it includes matters of "ought" as well as matters of "is"; and that the debate over those "oughts" is accessible to all men and women of good will, regardless of denominational affiliation (or the lack thereof). In this sense, the Finnis volume is a leap beyond moral emoting, a return to the classic canons of genuine moral argument, and a contribution to the reconstruction of a Western political culture capable, again, of arguing intelligibly about issues of great moral import. For all of this, we may be grateful.

But do Finnis, Boyle, and Grisez point a wise and persuasive way beyond the moral and political confusions of the present debate over the morality of nuclear weapons and strategy? Here, one is less inclined to be celebratory. The authors' sense of the historical contingencies engaged in the deterrence debate is insufficient. Moreover, *Nuclear Deterrence, Morality and Realism* has a maddening sense of "well, that settles that" about it. The entire thrust of the book is to end, once and for all, the moral debate over nuclear weapons and strategy. The authors believe, with commendable self-confidence, that they have built an unassailable moral case against deterrence. The argument over ethics and deterrence is likely to continue, however (a point the authors concede); thus, their book is more accurately described as defining one distinctive pole of the debate, rather than definitively settling the argument. On the other hand, the rigor with which that pole is defined and defended bids fair to shift the correlation of forces within the morality-and-deterrence argument. At a minimum, this will place great pressure on American political culture's willingness to sustain the deterrence system, even as an interim measure; and at a maximum, it could become the crucial point of transition by which the highest teaching authority of Roman Catholicism begins to consider rejecting the deterrence system as inherently immoral.[7] Thus even those who consider the authors' unilateralist policy prescription beyond the present boundaries of reasonable discourse have a great stake in engaging their moral argument.

Attending to History

Finnis and his colleagues argue that Western strategic policy is caught on the horns of a dilemma. Nuclear deterrence has indeed been a factor in preventing nuclear war; absent deterrence, the authors argue, Soviet hegemony in one form or another will be a fact of life. But this brutal result must be accepted. For the logic of the deterrence system involves the intention to murder innocents. Thus the authors resolve the dilemma by eliminating one side of it and taking the consequences. Their bottom line could (and doubtless will, by some activists) be reduced to a simple slogan: Just say no.

Nuclear Deterrence, Morality and Realism examines a host of proposals for moderating the deterrence system and finds all of them wanting. Arms control may be desirable, but because it, too, is based on the final threat of annihilative nuclear retaliation, it points no true way out. Albert Wohlstetter's and William V. O'Brien's proposals for an evolution toward low-yield, high-accuracy nuclear weapons that meet the just war criteria of proportionality and discrimination are illusory, because any deterrent based on them would still rely on massive numbers of civilian deaths as the deterring threat. Strategic defenses, even if technologically feasible, are so far in the future as to be no real factor in today's moral calculus. The West will never pay the price for a conventional deterrent that could checkmate the Warsaw Pact. And thus the hard choice remains—an immoral deterrent that may prevent war, or effective surrender to Soviet power and purposes.

There are several crucial factors missing, or inadequately accounted for, in this historical picture. In the first, and perhaps most important, instance, the authors do not convincingly confront the probability that unilateral nuclear disarmament by the West (or even by the United States) would lead, not simply to Soviet hegemony, but to nuclear war. For the deterrent has not merely prevented war between the United States and the Soviet Union, or between NATO and the Warsaw Pact. It has helped prevent nuclear war between the Soviet Union and the People's Republic of China. Given Soviet anxieties about the PRC, unilateral U.S. nuclear disarmament could well create conditions for a preemptive nuclear attack on Chinese military (and, quite probably, civilian targets) by the Soviet Union. The principal barrier against such an attack would be gone. Thus Finnis and his colleagues cannot argue that, whatever its other unfortunate consequences, "unilateral disarmament by the U.S. or by all the Western powers . . . if done in such a way as to leave Soviet power unopposed, would very probably avoid nuclear war. . . . " It would do no such thing. It would, in fact, make nuclear war more, rather than less, likely.[8]

I raised this point with Bishop Thomas Gumbleton during my 1982 testimony before the Bernardin committee. The bishop asked why I, as someone who had spent (at that point) five years as a full-time professional in the peace business, rejected unilateralism. "Suppose," I asked the bishop, "I could convince you that a likely outcome of your unilateralist prescription would be a nuclear war between the Soviet Union and China. Would that change your prescription?" There was no answer from Bishop Gumbleton, and there is no satisfactory answer on this point from Finnis, Boyle, and Grisez.

On the contrary, Finnis and his colleagues offer the following summary: "The reality here is twofold: the menace of Soviet power if it were undeterred by a deterrent system such as actually exists; and the threat to kill the innocent, with its underlying intent, and its guilt."[9] But is that the reality?

More than our own consciences and skins are at stake

in deterrence. More than the freedom of the West, more than the grim prospect of a world under Leninist hegemony, is involved. Yes, of course, the Soviets would not invade a Western Europe whose economy they would wish to exploit (a point granted by the authors). But that is not the end of the matter, given the profound threat that the Soviet regime believes exists on its southern frontier–a belief that will continue, given demographic realities, no matter what modest degree of rapprochement is reached between Gorbachev's USSR and Deng Xiaoping's PRC. Thus Western or U.S. unilateralism almost certainly means war, and most probably nuclear war. Nuclear death would result for millions of Chinese and, most probably, for millions of Soviets. This probability is insufficiently considered in the historical analysis of Finnis and his colleagues. The situation they portray is incomplete. Things are actually worse than they think, insofar as the likely results of unilateralism are concerned.

Similar questions should be raised about Finnis's failure to confront thoroughly the relationship between deterrence and nuclear proliferation. A nuclear weapon has not been fired in anger since August 9, 1945. Given the realities of the Indo-Pakistani conflict, the fact of a nuclear-capable India, and Pakistan's efforts to match that capability; given the turmoil of the Middle East, and the evidence from the Iran-Iraq war that fanaticism indeed leads to the use of horrific weapons of indiscriminate destructiveness; given the situation of South Africa; given the nonadherence of Brazil and Argentina to the Nuclear Non-Proliferation Treaty–given all of this, our authors' lack of detailed attention to the virtually inevitable proliferation that would follow the unilateral nuclear disarmament of the West has about it a very troublesome historical insouciance. One suspects that this is not what Finnis, Boyle, and Grisez intend, but that is what they communicate.

The authors' account of the calculations by which the Soviet leadership is checked by the Western deterrent is also unsatisfactory. "What the West desires the Soviets to fear includes many deaths of innocents," argue the authors; because the Soviets do fear this, they are thereby deterred.[10] But is this quite right?

During the past 70 years, the leadership of the Soviet Union has not exhibited a marked disinclination to sacrifice innocents when this would advance the interests of the Soviet *nomenklatura* elite. From Lenin's Cheka through Stalin's purges, anti-kulak collectivization schemes, and the Ukrainian terror famine, and on through the political abuse of psychiatry during the Brezhnevian "period of stagnation," Leninist leaders have proven time and again that the strategic bottom line involves maintaining their own privilege and power. (Whether this is still argued, among the *nomenklatura*, in terms of a Marxist worldview and the historical role it assigns to the Communist Party is irrelevant.) The reforms of the Gorbachev era notwithstanding, there is virtually no evidence to indicate that this strategic calculus has changed. What this suggests is that deterrent forces aimed at Soviet citizens are rather less likely to deter than a deterrent that places at risk those Soviet military and political assets by which the *nomenklatura* maintains its control. Recognizing this does not, of course, settle the moral argument, because issues of what strategists so pristinely refer to as "collateral damage" would remain. But it does suggest that the city-busting basis of deterrence argued for by the authors may not be, in reality, what in fact deters.

"Common Morality" and Deterrence

The truly radical quality of *Nuclear Deterrence, Morality and Realism* comes into clearer focus if one recognizes that its authors might well concede the flaws in their historical account, and then say, in effect, "So what?" Perhaps the Soviet leadership calculates "unacceptable damage" in terms other than our own. Perhaps the result of Western or

U.S. unilateral nuclear disarmament would be some form of nuclear war – not Armageddon, but something very bad indeed. Perhaps the result would be a massively irradiated China and a Soviet Union with several principal cities reduced to radioactive rubble. According to the authors, to give these probabilities any weight in the moral analysis of deterrence is to engage in "consequentialism." And concern for consequences is not to be countenanced, to any determinative degree, in the "common morality" as conceived by Finnis, Boyle, and Grisez.

This is not the place to review the past generation of intellectual combat over methods of moral reasoning in Roman Catholicism. Suffice it to say that *Nuclear War, Morality and Realism* has to be understood as part of the authors' larger attack on "consequentialist" ethics, a battle that they have vigorously engaged for many years, and in which they have made significant contributions to both philosophical and theological ethics. Moreover, one does not have to be an aficionado of the trench warfare among contemporary Catholic ethicists to have an instinctive appreciation of the appeal of our authors' radical critique of consequentialism. On December 7, 1987, for example, page one of the *Washington Post* offered an extraordinary example of consequentialism compounded by moral emotivism run riot; the headline in question read, "A Need Examined, a Prayer Fulfilled: Unmarried Priest Bears Child by Artificial Insemination." That consequentialism of this deracinated sort has been a major factor in the debasement of public moral discourse in America is, to me, beyond dispute. The question, therefore, is not whether radically consequentialist forms of ethics – devoid of any concern for the moral nature of the acts in question or the moral character of the actor – are bad news, both for ethics and for our public moral culture. The question engaged by Finnis turns on the issue of whether there is any room for calculations of consequence in the "common morality," or in any form of natural law reasoning. If there is not, then the capacity of natural law styles of moral reasoning to provide an ecumenical grammar for public moral argument in a pluralistic democracy is going to be constrained indeed.

There is one tactic for avoiding this issue, in a Catholic context, and that is to appeal to ecclesiastical authority. One could argue that, because Pope John Paul II has accepted deterrence as an interim arrangement that can be morally accepted insofar as it creates the stable conditions for the pursuit of mutual disarmament, the issue is settled for those who acknowledge the pope's authority. To buttress this argument, one could reexamine the minutes of the Vatican consultation on nuclear strategy of January 1983, which fell between the second and third drafts of "The Challenge of Peace" and was an important influence on the final outcome of that document. The consultation minutes indicate that the Cardinal Secretary of State Agostino Casaroli, and others, offered an argument that included a calculation of consequences (that is, loss of freedom under Soviet hegemony) in defending a conditional moral acceptance of deterrence. The Vatican plainly accepted deterrence as a stabilizing mechanism creating conditions for the pursuit of both peace and freedom, and the Vatican rejected unilateralism at least partly because of its likely consequences in respect of what were considered moral goods.[11]

But such an appeal to ecclesiastical authority is not very satisfactory. Although it is arguably true that the Catholic debate on the morality of deterrence will, given both its intellectual sophistication and the cultural weight of the Catholic bishops, have a more decisive effect on the wider public than the efforts of other religious leadership groups, the fact remains that the highest teaching authority of the Roman Catholic Church is not recognized as such by three-quarters of the American people. Moreover, and strictly within the Catholic context, one has to concede that the teaching authority could change its mind. That John Finnis is an active member of the Vatican's International Theological Commission as well as a consultor to the Vatican's Justice and Peace Commission suggests that such a change of mind is not entirely beyond the realm of possibility, if not now, then in the future. Thus the claim by Finnis and his colleagues that considerations of consequence are of little account in a moral analysis of deterrence conducted through the prism of the "common morality" must be engaged at a deeper level.

The question of consequences raises the question of the historicity of natural law reasoning. One often finds natural law moral theories dismissed by either the uncharitable or the uninformed as "ahistorical." According to the regnant caricature, natural law principles float in a sort of eternal ether, from which they are applied, without much exegetical fuss and bother, to the contingencies of the human condition. Perhaps in some cases the caricature speaks a measure of truth. But one could argue, even in the days before lesbian Episcopalian priests had babies by artificial insemination and justified this on consequentialist grounds, that natural law morality offered a far more textured and rich mode of moral reasoning than the caricature allowed.

Just war theory is a prime example of this. As its many contemporary critics on the political and theological left are eager to point out, the just war tradition did not, and does not, offer apodictic answers to the dilemmas of statecraft. Just war theory has always been understood, and should be understood today, as a calculus rather than an algebra. To mix the metaphor, the statesman reasoning according to the canons of just war theory is more like a conductor interpreting a symphonic score than an engineer factoring a quadratic equation. This was not, in the classic understanding of these things, a weakness of the just war tradition, but a strength. Human affairs are incorrigibly messy, and a moral system that pretends otherwise is certain to make a hash of both morality and public policy.

Such was the argument of John Courtney Murray, who explored the complex relationship between natural law moral reasoning and human historicity in these terms:

St. Thomas, of course, had quite clearly in mind that "man" is not an abstract essence but an historical existent, who does not act in a vacuum of space and time, at the same time that he must always act as a man, and not as an animal or an angel. . . . History does not alter the basic structure of human nature, nor affect the substance of the elementary human experiences, nor open before man wholly new destinies. Therefore history cannot alter the natural law, insofar as the natural law is constituted by the ethical *a priori*, by the primary principles of the moral reason, and by their immediate derivatives. History has not, for example, abolished the Ten Commandments.

But history, as any history book shows, does change what I have called the human reality. *It evokes situations that never happened before. It calls into being relationships that had not existed.* . . . In a word, it has been abundantly proved in history that the nature of man is an historical nature. "The nature of man is susceptible of change," St. Thomas repeatedly states. History continually changes the community of mankind and alters the mode of communication between man and man. . . . In this sense, the nature of man changes in history, for better or for worse; at the same time that the fundamental structure of human nature, and the essential destinies of the human person, remain untouched and intact.

As all this happens, continually new problems are being put to the wisdom of the wise; at the same time, the same old problems are being put to every man, wise or not. The basic issue remains unchanged: what is man or society to do, here and now, in order that personal or social action may fulfill the human inclination to act according to reason.[12]

Man's "inclination to act according to reason" is the heart of the issue. Many readers of *Nuclear Deterrence, Morality and Realism* will sense that there is something intuitively unreasonable about a moral argument whose conclusions include a concession that terrible things are likely to occur if the counsel of the ethicist(s) in question is taken. Has human reason been driven into such a cul de sac that it can only direct us to profoundly and even morally undesirable ends? This will seem especially odd when the moral judgment leading to those undesirable ends has to do, not with an action per se (that is, firing a nuclear weapon into a population center), but with a deterrence system whose primary purpose is to prevent such an outcome.

Thus, and despite their commendable efforts to inform themselves about both deterrence strategy and the exigencies of contemporary world politics, Finnis, Boyle, and Grisez seem perilously close to that ahistorical abstractness with which its enemies are wont to attack natural law morality. But is the form of natural law reasoning found in *Nuclear Deterrence, Morality and Realism* all there is in that venerable and rich tradition? According to classic Thomistic understandings, natural law morality emerges from reflection on real human situations. It does not, like Kantian principles, reside somewhere beyond immediate human experience. And in Thomistic natural law morality, consequences are surely in play. Most moral actions are intended to bring about a desirable set of circumstances, and thus to have consequences. Finnis and his colleagues seem to argue that any moral reasoning which recognizes a dialectic of intentions, acts, and consequences inevitably collapses into a utilitarian calculus. That is not the understanding, however, of a host of other Thomistically grounded ethicists.

Disputed Questions

Nuclear Deterrence, Morality and Realism has driven the moral debate over deterrence back to where it ought to have begun in the 1980s — that is, at the first principles of moral reasoning. Those principles have been difficult to discern in the welter of ecclesiastical "prudential judgments" about weapons and tactics that has shaped the religious community's nuclear debate in this decade. Thus the authors have done a most valuable service by forcing this argument down to its deepest roots. But they have not settled the argument, and as it continues (as it most assuredly will), the following points will be worth exploring.

1. Finnis and his colleagues do not give us a finally satisfactory account of the *intentionality* involved in the deterrence system. One intends many things by deterrence, but for any reasonable person the central and guiding intention of the deterrence system is to prevent nuclear war. No doubt there are many other levels of intentionality involved in so complex a phenomenon as deterrence. For deterrence is a system concretized in many acts – from research and development, to voting on appropriations, to building weapons, to training missile crews. If this system is judged as a whole, the reduction of what is "intended" to the alleged threat to do murder does not constitute a complete moral account of a complex reality in which many intentions are involved. Is there, in other words, a "hierarchy of intentions" involved in the deterrence system that would raise question about the rejectionist posture of Finnis and his colleagues?

Michael Novak's cut at this problem should be recalled:

It is clear that the complexities of nuclear deterrence change the meaning of "intention" and "threat" as these words are usually used in moral discourse. Those who intend to prevent the use of nuclear weapons by maintaining a system of deterrence in readiness for use do *intend* to use such weapons, but only in order *not* to use them, and do *threaten* to use them, but only in order to *deter* their use. That this is not mere rationalization is shown by the fact that several generations of nuclear weapons systems have become obsolete and been retired, without ever having been used. These are considered successful and moral systems. In the same way, deterrence is judged to be successful insofar as nuclear war does not occur.[13]

The authors contest Novak's understanding of intention, but there is considerable room for further discussion here, not only on the special moral grammar of "intent to deter," but particularly on the question of the complex of intentions involved in maintaining this deterrent of a type "hitherto unthought of."[14]

2. The *distinction between action and inaction* that Finnis and his colleagues seem to make also bears examination and debate. Our authors consider that maintaining a deterrent is an action for which we are responsible. They consider unilateral disarmament a cessation-of-action, whose consequences are not within the boundaries of our moral responsibility (the bad things to follow would be done by the Soviets, not by the West). But is there not some moral responsibility involved in creating (by cessation-of-action) conditions for the possibility of evil outcomes? We rightly judge Chamberlain and other appeasers of the 1930s to be partly responsible for the horrors of World War II. Their inaction created conditions that made possible Hitler's evil actions. Would Western governments not incur a moral burden similar to Chamberlain's if they adopted our authors' unilateralism – and particularly if unilateral disarmament made rapid nuclear proliferation and indeed nuclear war more, rather than less, likely? The human universe of moral deliberation and action is a historical universe. There are no hermetically sealed categories labeled, respectively, "morality" and "history." The distinction between action and inaction (or cessation-of-action) made by Finnis and his colleagues may lead them toward precisely this kind of bifurcated human universe.

3. Is the *relationship between personal conscience and public responsibility* suggested by our authors' anticonsequentialist reasoning sustainable? A pure conscience is a private good. But a single-minded focus on the demands of personal conscience can lead to public moral incoherence. Suppose, for example, that exercising personal conscience in pursuit of a private good results in destroying the society that protects that private good and gives scope for its pub-

lic exercise. Are we, in effect, making reservations for the catacombs here, with the elect shunning public responsibilities for the sake of preserving the private good of a conscience cleared of all ambiguities? This runs against the grain of modern Catholic social thought, with its teaching that the believer is to be a leaven transforming the affairs of this world. The approach of Finnis and his colleagues thus risks making Christian participation in politics impossible.

Moreover, is there a radical, and decidedly un-Catholic, moral individualism at work here? The authors make a sharp disjunction. They acknowledge the public good of freedom (that is, "the West's *moral responsibility* to preserve its independence against Soviet power").[15] Yet they also reject deterrence because deterrence violates an absolute norm that must inform individual conscience. Does this disjunction not, in a dramatic way, take the Christian out of history, indeed out of society? The authors might well reply that even obligatory ends cannot be pursued by immoral means. But this simply returns the argument to the question of intentionality in deterrence. The moral dilemma of deterrence is not immediately resolved by an appeal to the demands of personal conscience.

4. John Langan, S. J., has raised an interesting question about the notion of "exceptionless norms" found in the volume:

> One can follow the line of the French bishops [in their 1983 pastoral letter, *Gagner le paix*] and separate the moral evaluation of the deterrent threat and [the moral evaluation] of the actions that are threatened.[16] This goes against the wrongful intentions principle that "one may not intend what one may not do," a principle that Finnis, Boyle and Grisez regard as an essential part of the common morality. One can do this by arguing that this principle is not exceptionless. Thus one can argue that in the new situation created by the development of weapons of mass destruction in a politically divided world there are good reasons why this derivative norm of common morality barring threats to

innocent life should be understood in a way that allows
for exceptions. This would not be equivalent to endors-
ing the actual taking of innocent lives. Rather, the just-
ifying point of the threat is precisely to protect both
innocent lives and a broad range of political and moral
values the defense of which is authorized by just war
theory.[17]

Langan's formulation rings true to Murray's claim that
history changes the "human reality," evoking both "situations that never happened before" and "relationships that
had not existed." The axiological approach of the authors
does not.

5. The bleakness of the *strategic options* posed by Finnis and his colleagues is quite probably misstated. The authors give insufficient attention to the tangled, but perhaps
promising, impact of strategic defense capabilities on possible strategic futures. Astrodome fantasies aside, the
evolution of defensive systems holds open the prospect of a
"common security" approach to the threat of nuclear annihi-
lation. In this new approach, the United States and the
Soviet Union would cooperatively manage a transition to a
strategic regime dominated by defensive, rather than offensive, capabilities.[18]

Only those committed fideistically to the orthodoxies
of arms control dogma will fail to see that the advent of defensive capabilities affords us the opportunity to reconcep-
tualize the entire strategic debate.[19] In this new environ-
ment, the protagonists could reopen the question of linkage
among nuclear and conventional force reductions, nuclear
and conventional force modernizations, and the evolution of
defensive capabilities. Curiously, on this point, the authors
seem to accept the arms controllers' unproven claim that
there can be no connections among arms control, arms reduction, the pursuit of strategic stability, and a managed
evolution of defensive capabilities. But the history of nuclear weapons negotiations during the 1980s suggests that
this dogmatic rejection of linkage has been overcome by

technological and political facts. Adopting the unilateralism of Finnis, Boyle, and Grisez would render all these promising developments moot. That is not, in and of itself, a definitive counterargument to their proposition. But it does illustrate what is lost when a prescription of "Just say no" is made without giving a calculation of consequences its necessary role in the argument.

6. Finally, one has to probe the relationship between *Nuclear Deterrence, Morality and Realism* and the contemporary Catholic and ecumenical debate over the pursuit of peace. As I argued in *Tranquillitas Ordinis*, the classic Catholic heritage taught that peace was a matter of dynamic and rightly ordered political community. The just war tradition thus contained within itself a *ius ad pacem* that created the moral horizon against which (and toward which) questions of the *ius ad bellum* and the *ius in bello* had to be addressed. This tradition has special force in a modern world marked by the twin threats of nuclear or totalitarian holocaust. Yet this expressly *political* conception of "peace" has too often gotten lost in the contemporary Catholic debate. On the one hand, nuclear weapons tend to be treated as kind of independent variable in world affairs (one current in "The Challenge of Peace"). On the other hand, grossly psychologized understandings of conflict and "peace" dominate the energizing centers of the Catholic activist community. Having abandoned the classic moral and *political* horizon of *tranquillitas ordinis*, the Catholic debate has tended to drift into either weapons-policy micromanagement (the relationship of which to "peace" is never entirely clarified), or into psychobabble. In both instances, what is needed is a *repoliticization* of the peace debate.[20]

Finnis, Boyle, and Grisez's volume is not of much assistance in this regard. Their mode of moral analysis is deliberately apolitical in its radical rejection of a consequential criterion in evaluating the morality of deterrence. And thus whatever the impact of *Nuclear Deterrence, Morality and Realism* in the scholarly community, the book will almost certainly reinforce the depoliticization and psychologization of the debate among activists. The authors cannot, of course, be held entirely responsible for what others may make of their work. But they must know that their sophisticated arguments will be vulgarized as they are reduced to placards. (The 1987 meeting of the National Conference of Catholic Bishops in Washington featured an elderly woman standing in front of the Capital Hilton carrying a sign that read, "It's a sin to intend to kill an innocent.") Thus our authors are under an obligation to spell out in far greater detail the relationship between their unilateralist prescription and the moral imperative to seek peace with freedom and justice. That imperative has, since Augustine, involved calculations about the proportionate and discriminate use of armed force, or the threat thereof, as well as about the consequences of not doing so. The nuclear weapons issue is one (admittedly pressing) question within that larger complex. This complex is not addressed directly by Finnis, Boyle, and Grisez, and so one ought to hope that they will turn their considerable talents to these larger horizonal questions in the future.

On Not Ignoring the Radical

A world hostage to the threat of nuclear war is not the world any reasonable person would choose. There is undoubtedly a moral obligation to think our way "beyond" deterrence, and to do so in a fashion that enhances the prospects for both peace and freedom.[21] Some would argue that such a path lies through an evolution and transformation of the deterrence system, a position that Finnis, Boyle, and Grisez forthrightly reject. But irrespective of how one finally judges the merits of their moral argument, all parties must concede that nuclear weapons have indeed placed unprecedented strains on the "common morality." That these strains will eventually register in U.S. public life is one certainty in a typically uncertain world.

Thus while the radical unilateralist position ought, in

my judgment, to be rejected, it cannot be ignored – particularly when it issues, not from European "Greens" or American ecclesiastics conducting jeremiads against "our nuclear idol," but from sober, serious, and sophisticated scholars who concede rather than minimize or ignore the totalitarian threat. The Finnis-Boyle-Grisez volume has crystallized a profound tension in our contemporary political culture. If politics is indeed a function of culture, and if the root of culture is religion, as Paul Tillich used to insist, then it is a grave error to dismiss out-of-hand the religious or philosophical radical's sense that things-as-they-are are seriously out of sync with things-as-they-ought-to-be, at least insofar as those "oughts" have been identified in the classic moral-political tradition of the West.

To acknowledge this is not to be driven to a unilateralist prescription. It is to be driven beyond unilateralism, into more morally and politically satisfactory acts of political and ethical imagination. Such acts of imagination remain to be carried out. But one should not doubt that they are urgently required. Reminding us of that fact is the lasting contribution of works such as *Nuclear Deterrence, Morality and Realism*.

4

Ethics Meets Strategy: U.S. Foreign Policy and the Democratic Prospect

Kvetching – that onomatopoetic Yiddish term for "chronic complaining" – seems to be a durable feature of the human condition. And the human propensity to *kvetch* applies to history as well as to personal circumstance. One tale has it that the first tablet translated at Sumer – the first bit of recorded history known to us – read, "Things just aren't the way they used to be."

The risk of being thought a terminal *kvetcher* notwithstanding, it is not difficult to build a persuasive case that the twentieth century has been the most brutal in history. To be sure, there are things about the twentieth century that are worth celebrating. Ours, after all, is the century of Einstein, Salk vaccine, Apollo 11, the eradication of smallpox, the "green revolution," and so forth. Still, one cannot help but think, as the third millennium of the common era fast approaches, that the more characteristic hallmarks of the twentieth century (viewed either from the ground up, or *sub specie aeternitatis*) have not been these wholly admirable accomplishments of the human spirit, but events and places with names like Passchendaele, Ekaterinburg, Cheka, Gulag, *Kristallnacht*, Auschwitz, Coventry, Dresden, Ma'alot, and the sundry slaughters of Cambodia, Burundi, the Iran-Iraq war, and the Ethiopian famine. Whether one assigns war or totalitarian politics the principal blame for making an abattoir of modern life (and, on the research of R. J. Rummel of the University of Hawaii, the case here is settled in favor, if such be the term, of totalitarianism), the fact remains that more than 155 million human beings have died "unnatural," violent deaths since 1900.[1] Little wonder, then, that questions of theodicy – the theological exploration of "Why does a good God permit evil?" – are a staple of contemporary religious reflection.

Which brings us, by way of what the medievals would have called the *via negativa*, to a more hopeful development in late twentieth century life – namely, the democratic revolution and its impact on U.S. foreign policy. On the theory that those who have looked most closely into the heart of our modern darkness have a special claim on our attention, Professor Rummel's reflections on his sanguinary survey are worth noting. Rummel writes:

> In no case have I found a democratic government carrying out massacres, genocide, and mass executions of its own citizens; nor have I found a case where such a government's policies have knowingly and directly resulted in the large-scale deaths of its people through privation, torture, beatings, and the like. . . . Absolutist governments are not only many times deadlier than war, but are themselves the major factor causing war and other forms of violent conflict. They are a major cause of militarism. Indeed, absolutism, not war, is mankind's deadliest scourge of all.
>
> In light of all this, the peaceful nonviolent fostering of civil liberties and political rights must be made mankind's highest humanitarian goal. Not simply to give the greatest number the greatest happiness, not simply to obey the moral imperative of individual rights, but because freedom preserves peace and life.[2]

Rummel's claim – that the road to peace, within and among nations – is at least partly dependent upon the advance and defense of democracy, is now widely shared in significant sectors of the U.S. policy community. Whether that claim is always combined with a commensurately sophisticated analysis of the ways and means of democracy-building, or of the multiple obstacles in its path, is surely debatable. But the fact remains that, in an era when "bipartisanship" is more often an incantation than an operating reality, the notion that U.S. foreign policy ought to take democratization in the world as one of its chief objectives enjoys broad and truly bipartisan support. The issue to be explored, then, is how this often intuitive agreement can be given a sound moral, empirical, and strategic foundation.

The Case for Democracy: Moral Considerations

The moral case for democracy has been made by some of the most impressive social ethicists of our time. Pride of place among them (at least in terms of a continuing impact on the U.S. foreign policy debate) should probably go to Reinhold Niebuhr, among whose many writings on the subject the following may be taken as representative:

> Ideally, democracy is a permanently valid form of social and political organization in which freedom and order are made to support, and not to contradict, each other. It does justice to two dimensions of human existence: to man's spiritual stature and his social character; to the uniqueness and variety of life, as well as to the common necessities of all men. An ideal democratic order seeks unity within the conditions of freedom; and maintains freedom within the framework of order.
>
> Thus the democratic strategy is two-fold. First, it contributes to the establishment of order and community through the non-violent arbitration and accommodation of social conflict. Second, it seeks to maintain freedom by making power responsible, checking the authority of government, and providing a form of social control over the leaders of society.[3]

As a theologian influenced by both Calvinist and Lutheran currents of thought, Niebuhr knew that democracy could become an object of idolatry, a false religion, in which "we identify our particular brand of democracy with the ultimate values of life."[4] There were many kinds of golden calves waiting to be worshiped, Niebuhr understood, and the particular danger of the democratic golden calf was that it "might actually become democracy's undoing," for "no historic institution . . . can survive a too uncritical devotion."[5] Still, on balance and considering the available alternatives, a critical moral case for democracy could be (indeed, had to be) sustained; or, as Niebuhr summed things up in his most famous aphorism, "Man's capacity for justice makes democracy possible; but man's inclination to injustice makes democracy necessary."[6]

The Roman Catholic case for democracy was historically slower in developing, but it is now being made at the highest authoritative levels of the Church. The 1986 Vatican "Instruction on Christian Freedom and Liberation," a response to the Latin American theologies of liberation (many of which had deprecated democratic forms of government as bourgeois formalism), put the case in these terms:

> There can only be authentic development in a social and political system which respects freedoms and fosters them through the participation of everyone. This participation can take different forms; it is necessary to guarantee a proper pluralism of institutions and in social initiatives. It ensures, notably by the real separation between the powers of the State, the exercise of human rights, also protecting them against possible abuse on the part of the public powers. No one can be excluded from this participation in social and political life for reasons of sex, race, colour, social condition, language, or religion. . . . When the political authorities regulate the exercise of freedoms, they cannot use the pretext of the demands of public order and security in order to curtail those freedoms systematically. Nor can the alleged principle of national security, or a narrowly

economic outlook, or a totalitarian concept of social life, prevail over the value of freedom and its rights.[7]

More recently, Pope John Paul II, in his 1987 encyclical *Sollicitudo Rei Socialis*, argued that democracy and development in the impoverished and formerly colonized world were interrelated:

> Development demands above all a spirit of initiative on the part of the countries which need it. . . . It is important then that as far as possible the developing nations themselves should favor the self-affirmation of each citizen, through access to a wider culture and a free flow of information. . . . [Developing] nations need to reform certain unjust structures, and in particular their political institutions, in order to replace corrupt, dictatorial and authoritarian forms of government by *democratic* and *participatory* ones. This is a process which we hope will spread and grow stronger. For the 'health' of a political community – as expressed in the free and responsible participation of all citizens in public affairs, in the rule of law and in respect for and promotion of human rights – is the necessary condition and sure guarantee of the development of 'the whole individual and of all people.'[8]

This remarkable papal endorsement of democracy finds its proximate intellectual roots in the Second Vatican Council's "Declaration on Religious Freedom," whose personalist analysis of the inalienable human right of religious liberty has been extended and developed by John Paul II's structural-political analysis of the institutions necessary if the right of religious freedom is to be protected in the concrete, rather than merely asserted in the abstract. Thus has the highest teaching authority of Roman Catholicism evolved from the days when Pope Leo XIII, rightly regarded as the creator of modern Catholic social teaching, could warn (in 1895) against any temptation to absolutize the American model of democratic pluralism in a confessionally neutral state.[9]

The Lutheran scholar Richard John Neuhaus has summed up the contemporary Christian moral case for democracy in these terms:

> The deep compatibility between Christianity and liberal democracy is grounded in democracy's institutional protection of religious freedom and freedom of conscience, the single most important component of justice in the ordering of political life. In both principle and practice, in the modern world, religious freedom is reasonably secured only in those societies that are, or aspire to become, liberal democracies.
>
> The needed argument [about morality and foreign policy on this matter of the democratic prospect in the world] must address the overwhelming empirical evidence that democracy . . . best advances other elements of justice and social good. As to peace, democracies do not engage in the massive killing of their own citizens and do not go to war with one another. As to equality, democratic societies that give priority to liberty over equality do better by both liberty and equality than do societies that give priority to equality over liberty. As to virtue, societies that give priority to freedom over virtue do better by both freedom and virtue because, by definition, virtue must be free or it is not virtue. As to material prosperity, the case for democratic capitalism is beyond reasonable dispute. And so the list of components of the common good might be extended, each item subjected to testing by the empirical evidence produced by societies that are liberal democracies and those that are not.[10]

Amidst this striking agreement across confessional lines on the moral superiority of democratic forms of governance, a word of caution is in order. Niebuhr, John Paul II, and Neuhaus are not to be understood as arguing that the democratic prospect – in America or in the world – is to be taken as a kind of divine mandate. All forms of human polity, according to these social ethicists, stand under judgment. The question is, which currently available forms of governance, under the conditions of modernity, recognize that fact in the ways in which they legitimate their governmental structure and conduct the public's business? Which forms of governance, in other words, are deliberately self-limiting, because they hold themselves open to judgment according to moral norms that transcend the polity (whether those norms are understood in explicitly religious terms or not)? That democracies do this (however poorly at times), and other forms of government in the modern world do not, is the foundation of the ecumenical moral case for democracy.

The Case for Democracy: Empirical Considerations

Such moral arguments would seem rather ethereal, of course, and perhaps of interest only to members of the theological guild, unless they had some connection to facts "on the ground" in the contemporary world. Happily for our argument, those facts are, like June in *Carousel*, "bustin' out all over."

We can begin, once again, on the *via negativa*. On the well-established principle that "hypocrisy is the homage that vice pays to virtue," the very fact that Communist societies feel impelled to style themselves "democratic" is some indication of the energizing power that the democratic ideal enjoys in the modern world. Moreover, that such hypocrisies can, over time, be turned against those who have perpetrated them is evidenced daily in the news reports pouring out of eastern and central Europe, and indeed out of the Soviet Union itself.[11] Here, the much maligned "Helsinki process" and the indigenous democratic forces within Stalin's extended empire have come together to hold Communist oligarchs accountable to the democratic social and political norms that they putatively espouse. Although it would be rash indeed to predict the future (much less the ultimate success) of the democratic ferment now churning in virtually all Warsaw Pact countries, it would seem that even Communist Party officials are conceding that the economic growth they desperately seek will be impossible without the evolution of what the dissident community in these countries calls "the civil society." This civil society, while not fully democratic by Western standards, would involve the ideological legitimation and institutionalized protection of such predemocratic building blocks as the distinction in practice between the party and the government, a considerably broadened sphere of cultural autonomy, the rule of law, and a far more independent judiciary than has been the pattern in the post–World War II experience of these countries. Moreover, although it would be foolhardy in the extreme to think of Mikhail Gorbachev as an *in vitro* democratic pluralist, even the general secretary of the Communist Party of the Soviet Union (CPSU) seems to have formed the conviction that several of the instruments of "bourgeois formalism" (fixed and limited terms of office, multiple candidates in elections, a wider franchise) may just be of some use in redressing the sclerotic condition of the *nomenklatura* in the USSR.

In a more positive vein, the rise of the democratic revolution in Latin America has been one of the salient facts of international public life in the 1980s. At the beginning of this decade, there were but six functioning democracies in Central and South America, and approximately 17 percent of the population of Latin American countries lived under democratic regimes. At the close of the decade, Latin America could claim fourteen democracies, which included among them almost three-quarters of the population of the continent.

Undoubtedly many of these young democracies are very fragile, and the pressures they experience from poorly performing economies, large external debts, narco-terrorism, the imperatives of job-creation for the young, and Marxist guerrilla movements should not be minimized. On the other hand, the social infrastructure of democracy is being solidified throughout Latin America: in democratic trade unions, in democratic education projects such as those mounted by Argentina's "Consciencia" movement, in a variety of democratically committed political parties spanning the ideological spectrum, in the linkage being made by Mario Vargas Llosa and others between democracy and entrepreneurship, and through the work of the Catholic Church.[12]

This last factor is particularly notable in that traditional Iberian Catholicism of the sort that dominated the colonial culture of the continent was not, to be charitable, entirely enthusiastic about democratic pluralism. But under the influence of the Second Vatican Council, the 1968 and 1979 meetings of the Latin American bishops at Medellín, Colombia, and Puebla, Mexico, and the proddings of the Vatican during the papacy of John Paul II, the formal leadership of Latin American Catholicism has aligned itself squarely behind the democratic revolution, despite both traditional authoritarian pressures (as in Chile and Paraguay) and the Marxist-oriented critiques of democracy mounted by various of the theologies of liberation. Indeed, on this latter score, one should note that the democratic experience in Latin America has impelled some of the more thoughtful liberation theologians to reassess their earlier deprecations of the democratic prospect.[13]

The democratic future in Latin America is by no means secured, and the failures of U.S. policy in Nicaragua may, sooner rather than later, directly threaten the nascent democracies of Central America, at the same time as economic pressures make the democratic case harder to sustain in countries like Peru.[14] The 1990s could well see some reverses in democratic fortunes in Latin America. But one can still argue that, at the close of the 1980s, a critical and self-reinforcing cultural mass in favor of democracy has been achieved in Latin America, such that the democratic revolution has a reasonable chance of being sustained over time despite occasional setbacks.

The 1980s have also witnessed democratic transitions

in East Asia—most dramatically in the Philippines and South Korea, less completely in Taiwan and Malaysia. The Philippines case is notable for its similarity to the Latin American situation, both in terms of promise and problems. The cases of South Korea and Taiwan are intriguing in a different respect, in that they illustrate ways in which successful economic development bears on democratization. As the sociologist Peter Berger has put it, "If capitalist development is successful in reaching economic growth from which a sizable proportion of the population benefits, pressures toward democracy are likely to appear."[15] This proposition certainly seems to have been empirically born out in South Korea and Taiwan and will be tested in a unique way in Singapore.

Berger does not believe that the currently available empirical evidence sustains another proposition—namely, that democracy is a necessary condition for successful economic development, as it was not in Meiji Japan or post-1953 South Korea. On the other hand, Berger acknowledges that some scholars have vigorously argued that "sub-political participation"—in village councils, farmers' associations, and so forth—may be a precondition to capitalism, given capitalism's "affinity with spontaneous institutions of participation," or "mediating structures" that "serve as bridges between private and public life."[16] Asia thus appears to be an important laboratory for clarifying the relationship between successful economic development and successful democratization in the 1990s: not only in reference to the new democracies of East Asia, but also in terms of the stability of such established democracies as India.

If a democratic revolution is under way in Latin America and parts of Asia, and if a predemocratic ferment is challenging the Marxist oligarchies of the Warsaw Pact in unprecedented ways, the same cannot, unhappily, be said of Africa. The entire sub-Saharan continent contains only one functioning democracy, Botswana, and throughout the rest of black Africa the trend seems to be toward one-party or military rule. There are exceptions to this general situation, however. According to the Hoover Institution's Larry Diamond, "Despite the lengthening shadow of the state over economic and social life in Africa, a rich and vibrant associational life has developed in many African countries independent of the state, and this pluralism in civil society has been one of the most significant forces for democracy."[17] Countries like Senegal and Kenya have witnessed a strengthening of predemocratic institutions (for example, independent judiciaries) during the past decade. And in Nigeria and Ghana, the plural institutions of a civil society have "repeatedly resisted and frustrated attempts to perpetuate authoritarian rule."[18]

Despite these signs of hope, however, the overall picture remains one of great difficulty for democratization, given tribalism, the rise of militant and fundamentalist Islam, and desperate economic circumstances. One might hope that, as the generation of Kenneth Kaunda, Julius Nyerere, and Felix Houphouët-Boigny passes from the scene, a successor generation, reflecting on the dismal failures of its elders, might look toward democratic institutions as one part of the answer to Africa's grinding poverty and chronic fissiparousness. But the current pattern, which seems to involve the replacement of one form of undemocratic governance by another (as in the Ghana of Jerry Rawlings or the Zimbabwe of Robert Mugabe), does not lead one to much short-term optimism about the formal structures of democratic politics in Africa.[19]

Nor should one expect a major democratic breakthrough in the Islamic world, in north Africa, the Middle East, or Asia. Here, perhaps the best that can be hoped for is the development and nurturance of such predemocratic institutions as the unelected but generally representative consultative councils found in the Gulf states. Morocco, in which democratic institutions are being sustained at the local government level, may be an exception to this general rule. Pakistan is another possible counter-case, but there the combination of ethnic and religious volatility, economic pressure, and Soviet destabilization efforts warn against too easy an optimism.

Still, and granted these areas of difficulty, the fact remains that something that can be reasonably called a "democratic revolution" seems under way throughout the world. Why has this happened? Carl Gershman, president of the National Endowment for Democracy, suggested five reasons in his organization's 1987 annual report:

> Allowing for the periodic reversals that are part of any complex and turbulent historical process, the movement toward democracy is likely to continue because
> • democratic systems are in the best position to respond in a timely and creative way to the rapidly changing conditions brought on by the accelerating revolution in science and technology;
> • the spread of popular democratic culture, with its demands for increased political participation, is a by-product of the increased accessibility of information that is part of the communications revolution;
> • the popular desire for economic growth and disillusionment with failed statist approaches has revived interest in market solutions to economic problems;
> • the spread of economic growth will inevitably produce a more educated and politically active population;
> • [and] with the sole exception of Islamic fundamentalism, utopian political ideologies are in decline — most notably Communism, which can no longer mobilize culturally active forces.[20]

Of all these factors, perhaps the most significant has been the communications revolution. Both traditional authoritarian and totalitarian regimes have been undermined by the ubiquity of such inexpensive and virtually uncontrollable instruments of international communication as transistor radios. The communications revolution has fed, in turn, a revolution of rising social expectations throughout the world. People now know that malnutrition, epidemics, high infant mortality rates, early death, and illiteracy are not in the nature of things – in the sense that each of these deprivations is susceptible of cure, when human imagination and identifiable skills are applied to relieving them. It is a short step from this recognition to the perception that one's government – be that a government of caudillos or commissars – is not applying those skills with nearly the degree of success found in both old and new democracies. Contrary to the theorists of "consciousness raising," poor people do know what's good (and bad) for them, without the ministrations of bureaucrats trained at the totem of Paolo Freire. Thanks to the communications revolution, they now have a window onto why achievable social, cultural, and economic goods are being denied them.[21]

Thus the advent of cheap radios, audio and video cassettes, and the other media of the modern communications revolution has led, inexorably, to the delegitimation of traditional authoritarian and totalitarian forms of government. From that delegitimation, pressures for democratization are born.

The Case for Democracy: Strategic Considerations

The foreign policy agencies of the U.S. government should not be considered analogous, on the level of international life, to state and local social welfare departments. Foreign policy, for precisely ethical reasons, cannot be disinterested policy.[22] In other words, the moral case for democracy, buttressed by the empirical fact of the democratic revolution throughout the world, must be completed by a strategic analysis. Why should democratization in the world be in the interest of the United States?

Four reasons suggest themselves.

First, if it is to draw the support of the American people, U.S. foreign policy must be seen to reflect the values that our own experiment in democratic republicanism holds most dear. Put another way, it is impossible to run U.S. foreign policy on realpolitik considerations alone. For better and for worse, and usually for both, the American people generally prefer that their government deal with the world in ways that seem congruent with the moral claims on which our own republic rests. Support for democratic forces in authoritarian and totalitarian countries meets this requirement, as open-ended support for authoritarians (General Thieu in South Vietnam, the Shah of Iran) did not.

Second, support for democratization complements U.S. economic assistance programs, whose potential success is jeopardized by political chaos in the recipient country. For economic assistance to fulfill its promise, a minimum of political stability is required in the developing nation in question. Democracies are more likely to provide political stability than traditional authoritarianisms, Marxist-Leninist systems, or the modern "national security state." Political aid aimed at developing democracy is thus an important adjunct to economic assistance.

Third, democratization is in the national security interest of the United States. In the modern world, the four traditional instruments of statecraft (military force, economics, diplomacy, and information-propaganda) have been complemented by a fifth: organizing political movements around the world that have an affinity with one's own values, in the hope that such movements will align themselves accordingly in the global balance of power. This organizational component of statecraft has been vigorously exploited by the Soviet Union in its post-1945 efforts to change the "correlation of forces" in world politics. Prudence requires a parallel effort from the developed democracies, and particularly from the United States.

Fourth, the advance of democracy strengthens the prospects for peace in the world. Put most simply, the more democracies there are, the less the chances of war, because, on the present historical record, developed democracies do not go to war with each other. Moreover, democracies conducting their domestic affairs according to the classic Western concept of peace as *tranquillitas ordinis* are more likely to seek to establish a measure of *tranquillitas ordinis* in international public life. Thus the growth of democracy throughout the world enhances the prospect that Augustine's "tranquillity of order," or, in modern terms, the peace of dynamic and rightly ordered political community, might become more of a reality among, and not simply within, nations.[23]

In short, overt U.S. support for nascent democracies and democratic reformists in authoritarian and totalitarian societies is one of those happy policies in which the national interest (in terms of economics, national security, and international order) and a sense of national purpose coincide.[24] That this congruence between interest and purpose is the foundation of creativity and success in U.S. foreign policy is nowhere better illustrated than in such achievements of the Truman administration as the Marshall Plan and NATO.

Advices and Cautions

It is beyond the scope of this essay to present in detail a complete policy of democratization in all its component parts.[25] What is perhaps more appropriate is to sketch a set of moral cautions and tactical priorities, which may be useful to those whose business it is to design U.S. policy in the rapidly expanding field of democratic assistance.

The first caution that must be raised is a caution against the classic American temptation to universalism. The goal of U.S. democratic assistance programs cannot be to recreate the world in our own sociocultural image and likeness, for there are many parts of the world that do not wish to be so reconstructed; and that desire has a moral weight that must be respected. Successful democratic transitions do not require that developing countries become ersatz Americas in all of their social and cultural attitudes and practices.[26] Nor can U.S. policy planners and policymakers insist that developing democracies quickly meet some absolute standard of democratic political purity that our own democracy, in truth, has failed to achieve in 200 years. Independent sector U.S. support for election monitoring and supervision (including support that uses congressional funding) is entirely appropriate, and usually welcomed by democrats in transition situations.[27] But there is something faintly absurd about politicians from Cook County or Fort Worth bathing in the glow of democratic rectitude and demanding simon-pure electoral practices in Third World countries. Such posturings embarrass the United States and demean the democratic process here and abroad. Our primary task is to help support local democrats in their efforts; it is not to play the recording angel.

The modesty of our approach should reflect the modesty of a minimalist definition of "democracy." Although one can find lengthy and complex discussions of the nature of "democracy" in texts of political theory and political science, Peter Berger is surely correct in arguing that all such discussions eventually reduce to two key points – whatever else it may mean, "democracy" means that you can throw the rascals out every now and then, and that there are limits to what the rascals can do when they're in power.[28] The pluralization of political power, and effective, institutionalized protections of basic human rights are thus the two structural goals that U.S. democratic assistance programs should try to help achieve. Given a firmness of commitment to these goals, U.S. policy can afford to be quite flexible about the forms of democracy. It would be silly, for example, for U.S. policy to be based on an insistence that the only true "democracies" have bicameral legislatures, or executive departments independent of the legislature, or quadrennial elections on the second Tuesday in November; mercifully, that kind of political proselytization seems unlikely to shape policy in the immediate future. On the other hand, the two goals just identified (throwing the rascals out occasionally, and limiting their power when they're in) require, for their pursuit, an independent judiciary, which is an indispensable building block of democracy in any conceivable circumstance.

Nor can U.S. policy assume that all presently nondemocratic states are in an equal position at the starting line toward democratization. To take but two recent Caribbean examples – Grenada was clearly better equipped for a successful democratic transition (despite having been ruled for some years by the Marxist-oriented New Jewel Movement) than Haiti, where the cultural, social, and economic building blocks of democracy (to say nothing of the political foundations for a democratic transition) had simply dissolved during the Duvalier years.

Haiti is an extreme case, but it does illustrate an important point: the path to successful democratization in the political arena requires the strengthening (where it exists) or the formation (where it does not) of what we might call a "democratic culture" in the country in question. This means that in countries now ruled by classic authoritarians, and in immediate "post-transition" situations (for example, the Philippines, South Korea), U.S. policy should place particular emphasis on programs of civic "education for democracy," and on strengthening those "predemocratic" institutions on which the democratic political superstructure will have to rest: the legal system (is it codified?); the police (are they adequately trained, so that their actions reinforce the notion of the "rule of law?"); the media (has an appropriate and dynamic balance been achieved between the right of freedom of the press and the responsibility of accurate reporting?); trade unions (are they democratic in their own internal life, and will they support the democratic political process even if it registers results that are distasteful?); chambers of commerce and other business associations (have they been freed from crippling, mercantilist state regulatory and licensing practices, and are they, like the unions, willing to abide by democratic political decisions that may go against their immediate interests?). U.S. policy should also take account of the urgent need for effective economic assistance to new democracies, in which the democratic future will greatly depend upon the ability to relieve situations of gross deprivation and achieve a sustainable pattern of economic growth. In situations where the new democracy is suffering under a massive external debt, debt-for-equity or debt-for-democracy "swaps" should be actively explored and instituted where feasible.[29]

In totalitarian states, the focus of U.S. democratization policy ought to be on efforts to rebuild the "civil society," which means strengthening those mediating religious, cultural, and social institutions that stand between the individual and the megastructure of the totalitarian state. Here may be found both the present sources of opposition to the economic, social, and political senility of Marxism-Leninism, as well as the building blocks for a possible democratic transition in the future.[30]

Beyond Evangelism

The kind of democratization policy envisioned here differs from Wilsonian evangelism in four key respects.

First, it chooses its targets carefully, understanding that different societies are at different "predemocratic" stages of social and cultural life. A policy grounded on the principle of "idealism without illusions" would realize that some situations are far more susceptible to democratization than others, and would concentrate its primary efforts on those transitional situations where a sufficient minimum of democratic culture exists to sustain and support democratic political institutions. The kind of policy envisioned here would acknowledge, forthrightly, that some societies are extremely unlikely candidates for democratization in the foreseeable future (one thinks of many Islamic states), as it would also acknowledge that, in some circumstances, the path from brutal authoritarianism to democracy may lie through a phase of benign authoritarianism (Haiti, perhaps).

Second, U.S. policy in the terms envisioned above would act in response to requests for aid from indigenous democratic forces in authoritarian or totalitarian states. It would go "where it was asked," so to speak, on the moral and strategic assumption that indigenous forces are best positioned to know what constitutes useful and appropriate democratic assistance in their own unique situation.

Third, U.S. policy as conceived here would respect local cultural differences and would assiduously avoid the omnipresent temptation to read all of reality through the prism of the American cultural and political experience. Its purposes would be to provide democratic political assistance; it would not conceive itself as an instrument of cultural evangelization.[31]

Finally, the kind of democratization policy that makes ethical and strategic sense would be one that recognized that democracy is not America's only objective in world politics. A national government's first responsibility is the security of its citizenry. But a case can be made that strengthening the democratic prospect in the world enhances U.S. national security—and indeed links the quest for security with the pursuit of peace in a way that just might, over time, help to reorder the American debate about the elements of a "strategy of peace" in this kind of a world. The lessons of the late 1970s in Nicaragua, where the failure to identify and support a democratic alternative to the authoritarian kleptocracy of Anastasio Somoza resulted in a transition from bad to worse, should be of particular interest to foreign policy realists—as should, from a more positive angle, the successful transition to democracy that now seems possible in Chile, where support for indigenous democrats preempted the capacity of the radical left to pose itself as the only post-authoritarian alternative.

The economic well-being of our people is another irreducible goal of U.S. foreign policy. But here, too, democratization can be of some assistance, because, as argued above, stable political conditions are one prerequisite for successful economic development.

Order in international public life is another essential goal of U.S. foreign policy. A morally sound and strategically sophisticated democratization policy will consider fully the problem of unintended consequences, and will be attentive to the possibility that even the best-intended policies can turn situations from bad to worse. The activist may enjoy a *frisson* of moralistic self-satisfaction when he blithely works to destablilize an authoritarian regime without regard for the possible consequences of his action. But such activities are not exercises in moral reasoning, properly understood, because moral argument on policy matters, where others' lives and well-being are at stake, must include a calculus of consequences. To raise such cautions is not to argue for timidity in the midst of volatile transition situations such as were present in the Philippines in the mid-1980s. It is to remind ourselves that order is a moral value, within and among nations. The democratic prospect is not enhanced when U.S. policy creates conditions for the possibility of a situation in which bad becomes worse. We ought to have learned something from the experience of Iran and, as suggested just above, Nicaragua in the late 1970s.

On the other hand, we ought not to have learned from those, and other, cautionary experiences that our opportunities to help the world's democrats are radically circumscribed. To the contrary, far more than in 1919, and far more than in 1945, the possibilities for effective U.S. democratic assistance in Second and Third World arenas are legion. The reasons for that encouraging development lie not primarily with ourselves, but with brave democrats in a host of difficult situations. Whether the United States can in fact aid those men and women in their efforts will be an important index of the degree to which Americans have learned the difference between moral*ism* and moral reasoning – the difference between proselytizing and strategy.

Notes

Chapter 1

1. John Courtney Murray, *We Hold These Truths: Catholic Reflections on the American Proposition* (Garden City: Doubleday Image Books, 1964), 7.

2. Charles Krauthammer, "Isolationism: A Riposte," *The National Interest* 2 (Winter 1985–1986): 155.

3. Peter L. Berger, "Different Gospels: The Social Sources of Apostasy," 1987 Erasmus Lecture of the Center on Religion and Society, New York, *This World* 17 (Spring 1987): 6–17.

4. Murray, *We Hold These Truths*, 263.

5. Ibid.

6. Stanley Hauerwas, unpublished manuscript, quoted in *American Purpose* 1, no. 3 (March 1987): 23.

7. See, for example, Krauthammer's essay "Morality and the Reagan Doctrine," *The New Republic*, September 8, 1986, pp. 17–24.

8. See Tucker's commentary on the Second Vatican Council's Pastoral Constitution on the Church in the Modern World, in *Just War and Vatican Council II: A Critique* (New York: Council of Religion and International Affairs, 1966).

9. See William V. O'Brien, *The Conduct of Just and Limited Wars* (New York: Praeger, 1981).

10. See my probe toward such a reconstruction in *Tranquillitas Ordinis: The Present Failure and Future Promise of American*

Catholic Thought on War and Peace (New York: Oxford University Press, 1987), chapter 13.

11. See Peter L. Berger, *The Capitalist Revolution: Fifty Propositions about Prosperity, Equality and Liberty* (New York: Basic Books, 1986); Peter L. Berger and Michael Novak, *Speaking to the Third World: Essays on Democracy and Development* (Washington, D.C.: American Enterprise Institute, 1985); William Douglas, *Developing Democracy* (Washington, D.C.: Heldref Publications, 1972).

12. J. Francis Stafford, "This Home of Freedom: A Pastoral Letter to the Archdiocese of Denver," 33 (pamphlet available from the Archdiocese of Denver).

13. See Timothy Garton Ash, "Does Central Europe Exist?" *New York Review of Books*, October 9, 1986, p. 45.

14. See Aaron Wildavsky, "Containment Plus Pluralization," in *Beyond Deterrence*, Aaron Wildavsky, ed. (San Francisco: Institute for Contemporary Studies Press, 1983).

15. See, for example, the September–October 1988 issue of "Religion and Democracy," the newsletter of the Institute on Religion and Democracy, for an analysis of the extraordinary theological and political confusions at work in the National Council of Churches' recent overtures toward North Korea.

16. Cited in Paul Ramsey, "Tucker's Bellum Contra Bellum Iustum," *Just War and Vatican Council II: A Critique*.

Chapter 2

1. Martin Stannard, *Evelyn Waugh: The Early Years 1903–1939* (New York: W. W. Norton, 1987).

2. Edmund Morris, "A Better Kind of Dust," *New York Times Book Review*, August 30, 1987, p. 1.

3. This reediting of the three original novels, which was undertaken for commercial purposes and which involved the elimination of a number of minor characters and scenes, as well as a slightly amended ending, is not generally regarded as a critical success, and it is the original editions of the three individually published novels that will be drawn on here.

Waugh's correspondence with his literary agent on the renaming of *Unconditional Surrender* for the U.S. edition offers some insight into the author's humor, his low regard for American critics, and his summary analysis of the moral meaning of the war:

> Titles . . . to choose from: "Depths and Shoals of Honour," "Shoals of Honour," "Peace without Honour," "Honour comes a pilgrim grey," "Guy Crouchback," "The End of the Battle," "Peace," "The Sword," "A Sword," "Quixote in Modern Dress." Or if he prefers it, "Uncle Tom's Cabin & the Seven Dwarfs."

In an earlier letter, Waugh had proposed the titles "Chivalry" and "Conventional Weapons," and asked, "What will help the poor reviewers to understand better? That's really all that matters." (Cited in *The Letters of Evelyn Waugh*, Mark Amory, ed. [New York: Penguin Books, 1980], 565.)

4. Christopher Sykes, *Evelyn Waugh: A Biography*, rev. ed. (New York: Penguin Books, 1977), 550.

5. Evelyn Waugh, *Men at Arms* (Harmondsworth: Penguin Books, 1964), 12.

6. Ibid., 20.

7. Ibid., 142.

8. Evelyn Waugh, *Officers and Gentlemen* (Harmondsworth: Penguin Books, 1964), 47.

9. Waugh, *Men at Arms*, 25.

10. Waugh, *Officers and Gentlemen*, 44.

11. Ibid., 122.

12. Ibid., 114.

13. Ibid., 240.

14. Evelyn Waugh, *Unconditional Surrender* (Harmondsworth: Penguin Books, 1964), 232.

15. Waugh wrote about the foibles of military bureaucracy from extensive personal experience. In November 1939, for example, while trying to enlist in the Royal Marines, he wrote a friend, "The Marines have sent me a long questionnaire asking among other things if I am a chronic bedwetter. It seems probable that I am going to get a commission there." (Cited in Sykes, *Evelyn Waugh: A Biography*, 272.)

16. In this judgment, Waugh anticipated the later scholarly research of John Keegan (*The Face of Battle*) and Paul Fussell (*The Great War and Modern Memory*).

It can be argued, of course, that "ever has it been thus"; did the Roman legionnaires at the Battle of Teutoburger Forest understand that they were participants in a struggle which eventually secured the barbarian enclave in central Europe—a result whose ramifications remain with us today? It seems unlikely. But Waugh, anticipating Fussell, may well be arguing the subtler point that modern organization for war deliberately obscures the larger issues of the conflict for the sake of bureaucratic efficiency.

17. Waugh, *Men at Arms*, 203, 218.
18. Waugh, *Officers and Gentlemen*, 31.
19. Cited in Sykes, *Evelyn Waugh: A Biography*, 560.
20. Waugh, *Officers and Gentlemen*, 172.
21. Ibid., 201.
22. Waugh, *Unconditional Surrender*, 63–64.
23. Waugh, *Officers and Gentlemen*, 79.
24. Ibid., 101.
25. Ibid., 73.
26. See, for example, Neville Braybrooke's review of Stannard's biography, "The Spectacle of a Literary Craftsman," *Commonweal*, October 23, 1987.
27. Waugh's Christian realism is nowhere better expressed than in the letter he wrote to the author Edith Sitwell on her reception into the Catholic Church:

> Should I as Godfather warn you of probable shocks in the human aspect of Catholicism? Not all priests are as clever and kind as Fr. D'Arcy and Fr. Caraman. (The incident in my book of going to confession to a spy is a genuine experience.) But I am sure you know the world well enough to expect Catholic bores and prigs and crooks and cads. I always think to myself: "I know I am awful. But how much more awful I should be without the Faith." One of the joys of Catholic life is to recognise the little sparks of good everywhere, as well as the fire of the saints. (*Letters of Evelyn Waugh*, 451.)

28. Waugh, *Men at Arms*, 13.
29. Waugh, *Unconditional Surrender*, 23.
30. Sykes, *Evelyn Waugh: A Biography*, 562.
31. Waugh, *Officers and Gentlemen*, 111.
32. Waugh's contempt for modern bureaucracy, and his sense of its perverse ability to blind unsuspecting and institutionally comfortable mandarins to the ideological nature of the conflicts in which they were in fact engaged, came together in this memorably sinister figure:

Sir Ralph Brompton had been schooled in the old diplomatic service to evade irksome duties and to achieve power by insinuating himself into places where, strictly, he had no business. In the looser organization of total war he was able to trip from office to office and committee to committee. The chiefs of HOO considered they should be represented wherever the conduct of affairs was determined. Busy themselves in the highest circles, they willingly delegated to Sir Ralph the authority to listen and speak for them and to report to them, in the slightly lower but not much less mischievous world of their immediate subordinates.

Liberation was Sir Ralph's special care. Wherever those lower than the Cabinet and the Chiefs of Staff adumbrated the dismemberment of Christendom, there Sir Ralph might be found. [*Unconditional Surrender*, 141.]

Cattermole incarnated, for Waugh, the tendency of the modern, secularized intellectual to fix his loyalties on a this-worldly faith:

When Major Cattermole spoke of the enemy he did so with the impersonal, professional hostility with which a surgeon might regard a malignant, operable growth; when he spoke of his comrades in arms [Tito's partisans] it was something keener than loyalty, equally impersonal, a counterfeit almost of mystical love as portrayed by the sensual artists of the high baroque.

"Officers and men," he proclaimed exultantly, "share the same rations and quarters. And the women too. You may be surprised to find girls serving in the ranks beside their male comrades. Lying together, sometimes, for warmth, under the same blanket, but in absolute celibacy. Patriotic passion has entirely extruded sex. The girl partisans are something you will never have seen before. In fact, one of the medical officers told me that many of them had ceased to menstruate. Some were barely more than schoolchildren when they ran away to the mountains leaving their bourgeois families to collaborate with the enemy. I have seen spectacles of courage of which I should have been skeptical in the best authenticated classical text. Even when we have anaesthetics the girls often refuse to take them. I have seen them endure excruciating operations without flinching, sometimes breaking into song as the surgeon probed, in order to prove their manhood. Well, you will see for yourself. It is a transforming experience."

Seven years previously J. Cattermole of All Souls had published *An Examination of Certain Redundances in Empirical Concepts*, a work popularly known as "Cattermole's Redundances" and often described as "seminal." Since then he had been transformed. [*Unconditional Surrender*, 165.]

33. Amory, ed., *Letters of Evelyn Waugh*, 443.

34. Ibid., 302.

35. Christopher Sykes, "Evelyn Waugh the Man," in *Good Talk: An Anthology from BBC Radio*, Derwent May, ed. (London: Victor Gollancz, 1968), 68.

36. Compare, for example, the 1987 encyclical *Sollicitudo Rei Socialis* 44. For an analysis of this development in Catholic social thought, see my essay, "The Democracy Connection," *This World* 22 (Summer 1988), 69–79.

37. Theodore M. Hesburgh, Foreword, in Jim Castelli, *The Bishops and the Bomb* (Garden City, N.J.: Doubleday Image Books, 1983), 11–12.

Chapter 3

1. John Finnis, Joseph M. Boyle, Jr., and Germain Grisez, *Nuclear Deterrence, Morality and Realism* (Oxford: Clarendon Press, 1987).

2. Quoted in Jim Castelli, *The Bishops and the Bomb: Waging Peace in a Nuclear Age* (Garden City, N.J.: Doubleday Image Books, 1983), 79.

3. The Vatican's unwillingness, in 1982, to consider unilateral nuclear disarmament as a viable moral option undoubtedly played a role in creating what I have called here the "Bernardin barrier." Still, I would judge that a primary concern of the committee was to keep the pastoral letter "in play" in the policy community, which would be impossible were the bishops to end up, as some members of the National Conference of Catholic Bishops as well as a host of Catholic activists devoutly desired, with a unilateralist prescription.

4. Bishop Gumbleton, a leader in Pax Christi-USA, had been a long-time activist for a host of causes and was a member of the bishops' drafting committee. Archbishop Hunthausen was prominent in the 1980s' debate for his description of the Trident submarine base at Bangor, Washington as "the Auschwitz of Puget

Sound." Bishop Matthiesen, in whose diocese the Pantex plant for the assembly of nuclear warheads was located, publicly urged those of his congregants employed at Pantex to seek other employment.

5. See the United Methodist Council of Bishops, "In Defense of Creation: The Nuclear Crisis and a Just Peace" (Nashville: Graded Press, 1986). The Methodist bishops were, evidently, even more eager than their Roman Catholic confreres to remain "in play" in the policy debate; how else could one explain the disjunction between their principled moral judgment (deterrence is idolatry) and their policy prescriptions (do arms control, even though the theory of arms control rests, at bottom, on mutual assured destruction as the *ultima ratio* of deterrence)?

6. See *Building Peace* (Washington, D.C.: National Conference of Catholic Bishops, 1988).

7. This was proposed and rejected at the Second Vatican Council. For the relevant history and commentaries, see *Commentary on the Documents of Vatican II, Volume Five, Pastoral Constitution on the Church in the Modern World*, Herbert Vorgrimler, general ed. (New York: Herder and Herder, 1969), Xavier Rynne, *The Fourth Session* (New York: Farrar, Straus, and Giroux, 1965), 225–230, and Vincent Yzermans, *American Participation in the Second Vatican Council* (New York: Sheed and Ward, 1967), 185ff.

8. Finnis et al., *Nuclear Deterrence, Morality and Realism*, 66. In a letter criticizing an earlier version of this essay (*Crisis*, April 1988, p. 9), John Finnis claimed that I misrepresented his and his colleagues' position on this point: "To demonstrate our 'insufficient sense of the historical contingencies,' [Weigel's] prize exhibit is our silence about the risks of nuclear war, e.g. between the Soviets and China, after unilateral U.S. nuclear disarmament. In fact, however, those risks are the *very first* we call to readers' attention. . . ." Professor Finnis then cited two passages from his book: "Unilateral disarmament by the U.S. . . . would not preclude the use of nuclear weapons by the Soviets, China, or other powers" (p. 66); "After unilateral nuclear disarmament by the West, nuclear weapons might well be used in at least three different sorts of context: in coercing the docile obedience or surrender of a conventionally armed West; in suppressing or punishing resistance in the new Soviet empire or sphere of influence; and in carrying on conflicts with warlords or factions within the new imperial order. In short, no one should presume that a Soviet dominated world

would be free from nuclear threats and nuclear destruction." (p. 67)

The ellipsis in Professor Finnis's first citation is instructive, as it excludes the phrase just cited in my text, namely, that unilateral disarmament *"would very probably avoid nuclear war."* Unless I cannot read the English language, that strikes me as a rather forthright prediction. As to the second citation, the point is not that the authors do not admit the *possibility* of the use of nuclear weapons by others after unilateral Western or U.S. nuclear disarmament; the point is that they do not sufficiently address the *probability* of such an outcome. Nor does the People's Republic of China fit the authors' sense of likely Soviet nuclear targets, i.e. "resistance" to the Soviet "sphere of influence" or "conflicts with warlords and factions within the new imperial order." A billion Chinese do not strike me, in all candor, as a "faction."

Later in their book, Finnis and his colleagues argue that the new Soviet "masters of such a world, no matter how brutal, would have no motive to risk destroying the whole world of which they were masters, nor even to wipe out their former adversaries whose resources and productive capacity they could freely exploit." (p. 67) Again, this does not seem a sufficient account of the realities of the Soviet-Chinese conflict, where the issue engaged is neither destroying the whole world nor seizing "productive capacity."

9. Finnis et al., *Nuclear Deterrence, Morality and Realism*, 161.

10. Ibid., 92.

11. For a further discussion of this important episode in the debate, see my *Tranquillitas Ordinis: The Present Failure and Future Promise of American Catholic Thought on War and Peace* (New York: Oxford University Press, 1987), 275–280.

12. John Courtney Murray, S. J., *We Hold These Truths* (Garden City, N.J.: Doubleday Image Books, 1964), 115–117.

13. Michael Novak, *Moral Clarity in the Nuclear Age* (Nashville, Tenn.: Thomas Nelson, 1983), 59.

14. See Finnis et al., *Nuclear Deterrence, Morality and Realism*, 202–203, and Vatican Council II, *Pastoral Constitution on the Church in the Modern World*, 81.

15. Finnis et al., *Nuclear Deterrence, Morality and Realism*, 75 [emphasis added].

16. English translation available in *Bishops' Pastoral Letters*, James V. Schall, S. J., ed. (San Francisco: Ignatius Press, 1984), 101–120.

17. John Langan, S. J., "Writing Straight with No Crooked Lines," *The Tablet*, December 5, 1987, pp. 1329–1330.

18. For a detailed analysis of this possibility, see my essay, "Breaking the Doctrinal Gridlock: Common Security and the Strategic Defense Initiative," in *This World* 16 (Winter 1987): 3–22.

19. Unhappily, among such congregants must be counted (to date) the U.S. Catholic bishops, at least insofar as their 1988 statement on the morality of deterrence is concerned.

20. For a more extended discussion on this point, see my *Tranquillitas Ordinis*, 393–395.

21. One interesting and recent example of this, unfortunately constrained by its subtextual adhesion to the orthodoxies of liberal arms control theory, may be found in Joseph S. Nye, Jr., Graham T. Allison, and Albert Carnesale, eds., *Fateful Visions: Avoiding Nuclear Catastrophe* (Cambridge: Ballinger, 1988). See also *Promise or Peril: The Strategic Defense Initiative*, Zbigniew Brzezinski, ed. (Washington: Ethics and Public Policy Center, 1986), and chapter 13 of my *Tranquillitas Ordinis*.

Chapter 4

1. According to Rummel's figuring, 35.7 million people have been killed in the wars of the 20th century, while 119.4 million people have been killed by their own governments: 95.2 million by Communist states, 20.3 by other antidemocratic states, 3.1 million by "partially free" states, and 0.8 million by free states. See Rummel's op-ed essay in the *Wall Street Journal*, July 7, 1986.

2. Ibid.

3. Harry R. Davis and Robert C. Good, eds., *Reinhold Niebuhr on Politics* (New York: Charles Scribner's Sons, 1960), 183.

4. Ibid., 190.

5. Ibid., 190–191.

6. Reinhold Niebuhr, *The Children of Light and the Children of Darkness* (New York: Charles Scribner's Sons, 1944), xiii.

7. Congregation for the Doctrine of the Faith, "Instruction on Christian Freedom and Liberation," March 22, 1986, 95.

8. John Paul II, *Sollicitudo Rei Socialis* 44, in *Aspiring to Freedom*, Kenneth A. Myers, ed. (Grand Rapids, Mich.: Wm. B. Eerdmans Publishing Co., 1988), 55–56 [emphasis in original].

9. See Leo XIII's encyclical to the American Catholic hierar-

chy, *Longinqua Oceani*, in *Documents of American Catholic History*, John Tracy Ellis, ed., vol. 2 (Wilmington, Del.: Michael Glazier, 1987), 502.

The bridge between Leo's teaching and John Paul II's was built in considerable part by the work of the late John Courtney Murray, S. J., intellectual architect of the Vatican Council's "Declaration on Religious Freedom." See my chapter on Murray in *Catholicism and the Renewal of American Democracy* (New York: Paulist Press, 1989). For a discussion of John Paul II's development of the Catholic theory of religious freedom, see my essay "Religious Freedom: The First Human Right," in *This World* 21 (Spring 1988): 31–45.

10. Cited in *American Purpose* 1, no. 6 (July–August 1987): 46.

11. Perhaps the most striking example of this phenomenon at the end of 1988 was the remarkable ferment in the Baltic states of Lithuania, Latvia, and Estonia. See "'We Are Not Waiting for Gorbachev' – Interview with Tiit Madisson," *Uncaptive Minds* 1, no. 2 (June–July–August 1988): 44–46; Jozef Darksi, "The Baltic Republics: Between Anti-Stalinism and Anti-Communism," *Uncaptive Minds* 1, no. 3 (September–October 1988): 25–28; "Opposition as Self-Defense: An Interview with Heiki Ahonen," *Uncaptive Minds* 1, no. 3 (September–October 1988): 28–32; and Peter Conradi, "Grass-roots Groups Transforming Baltics," *Washington Times*, October 25, 1988, p. 1.

12. See the interview with Mario Vargas Llosa in *World Policy Journal* 4 (Fall 1988): 759–770. See also Hernando de Soto, *The Other Path* (New York: Harper & Row, 1989).

13. See, for example, the remarks of Father Gustavo Gutierrez of Peru, the founding father of liberation theology, in the *New York Times*, July 27, 1988. According to Peter Steinfels, religion editor of the *Times*, Father Gutierrez's theological movement is now "looking beyond social and economic conflict, relying less on Marxism, focusing more on spirituality and rethinking its attitudes toward democracy and socialism."

One of the more interesting phenomena to watch in the Latin America of the 1990s will be the continued growth of evangelical and fundamentalist Protestantism throughout the region, and the relationship between that phenomenon and the democratic revolution.

14. The irony here, of course, is that the economic failures of

military governments during the recessions of the 1970s helped clear the way for the democratic renaissance of the 1980s.

15. Peter L. Berger, *The Capitalist Revolution: Fifty Propositions about Prosperity, Equality, and Liberty* (New York: Basic Books, 1986), 84.

16. Ibid., 85.

17. Larry Diamond, "Introduction," *Democracy in Developing Countries: Africa* (Boulder: Lynne Rienner Publishers, 1988), 23.

18. Ibid.

19. One cultural variable that could conceivably accelerate the process of democratization in parts of sub-Saharan Africa is the tremendous growth rate of both Roman Catholicism and evangelical Protestantism throughout this vast region. In Zaire, Kenya, Tanzania, and Nigeria, for example, there are 128 Catholic bishops, a remarkable increase over the past generation. A countervariable to this, of course, is the parallel growth of militant and fundamentalist Islam in black Africa. The clash between these two religious forces – the Christians generally supporting democratization, and the fundamentalist Moslems generally hostile to it – is no theoretical matter, but is actually being played out "on the ground," in areas such as northern Nigeria.

20. Carl Gershman, "President's Report," *National Endowment for Democracy Annual Report 1987*, p. 5.

21. Three of Peter Berger's 25 theses in his 1974 study, *Pyramids of Sacrifice*, read as follows:

> 12. Policies for social change are typically made by cliques of politicians and intellectuals with claims to superior insights. These claims are typically spurious.
>
> 13. It is, in principle, impossible to "raise the consciousness" of anyone, because all of us are stumbling around on the same level of consciousness – a pretty dim level.
>
> 14. Every human being knows his own world better than any outsider (including the expert who makes policy).

On "consciousness-raising," Berger has this to say:

> A good way to begin a critique of the concept is to concretize it sociologically: *Whose* consciousness is supposed to be raised, and *who* is supposed to do the raising? The answer is clear wherever the term is used in political rhetoric: It is the

consciousness of "the masses" that must be raised, and it is "the vanguard" who will do the job. But who are these people? "The masses" are, of course, whatever sociological category has been assigned the role of the revolutionary proletariat by the ideologists of the putative revolution—industrial workers (in countries where this particular assignment still seems plausible), peasants, landless rural laborers, even white collar "wage slaves" or students. The "vanguard" consists of the aforementioned ideologists—typically intellectuals, who for our purposes may be defined here as individuals whose main preoccupation in life is the production and distribution of theories. Such individuals have usually passed through a long period of formal education, and usually come from the upper middle or upper classes of their societies. The concretization, therefore, may be put this way: "Consciousness-raising" is a project of higher-class individuals directed at a lower-class population. It is the latter, *not* the former, whose consciousness is to be raised. What is more, the consciousness at issue is the consciousness that the lower class has *of its own situation.* Thus a crucial assumption of the concept is that lower-class people do not understand their own situation, that they are in need of enlightenment on the matter, and that this service can be provided by selected higher-class intellectuals. . . .

"They don't understand what is good for them," is the clue formula of all "consciousness raising," of whatever ideological or political coloration—and "we do understand" is the inevitable corollary. Put differently, the concept allocates different cognitive levels to "them" and to "us"—and it assigns to "us" the task of raising "them" to the higher level. Coupled with this epistemological arrogance is a recurrent irritation with "those people" who stubbornly refuse the salvation that is so benevolently offered to them: "How can they be so blind?" [Ibid., 123–124]

Berger's critique of "consciousness-raising" is worth citing at such length because this seductive and dangerous concept is a crucial ideological component of the resistance to democratization among certain currents in the Latin American, African, and Asian variants in the theology of liberation, many of which have been deeply influenced by the politicized epistemology of Paolo Freire. Democracy inevitably means letting "those people" determine the future—and this, one has to say in all candor, does not seem to be to the taste of liberation theologians who dismiss democratic institutions of governance as "bourgeois formalism." In Latin America, in particular, the classic Iberian Catholic fondness for authoritarianism remains – although it is now transposed from the hierarchy to the intellectuals, and from the right to the left of the political spectrum, through the mediation of such liberation theologians as Juan Luis Segundo and Jon Sobrino.

22. The ethical reasons in question here have to do, of course, with the fiduciary and trusteeship roles of the government, which constitute a moral, and not merely practical, responsibility on the part of those who guide our national community in its intercourse with other national communities.

23. For a more complete discussion of peace as *tranquillitas ordinis*, see my *Tranquillitas Ordinis: The Present Failure and Future Promise of American Catholic Thought on War and Peace*, 357–371.

24. See my essay, "The National Interest and the National Purpose," in *This World* 19 (Fall 1988).

25. For a discussion of key elements of such a policy, see *Promoting Democracy: Opportunities and Issues*, Ralph M. Goldman and William A. Douglas, eds. (New York: Praeger, 1988).

26. This is particularly true in terms of U.S. population-control policy, which, according to some analysts, is bitterly resented throughout Africa, Asia, and Latin America.

27. The funding role played by the National Endowment of Democracy prior to the 1988 Chilean plebiscite is a model of how this can be done sensibly and effectively.

28. See Peter Berger, "Religious Liberty – *Sub Specie Ludi*," unpublished paper delivered at the National Symposium on the First Amendment Religious Liberty Clauses and American Public Life, held at the University of Virginia, April 11–13, 1988.

29. On "debt swaps," see Rose Gutfeld, "Banks Are Offered Way to Write Off Third World Loans," *Wall Street Journal*, November 19, 1987.

30. For discussions of the "civil society" in the eastern bloc, see Timothy Garton Ash, "Does Central Europe Exist?" *New York Review of Books*, October 9, 1986, and S. Frederick Starr, "Soviet Union: A Civil Society," *Foreign Policy* 70 (Spring 1988): 26–41.

31. For a cautionary tale on this point, see Owen Harries, "'Exporting Democracy'– and Getting it Wrong," *The National Interest* 13 (Fall 1988): 3–12.

Index

Action, vs. inaction, 53
Africa, 68–69, 89*n*.19
Americans for Democratic Action, 5
Aquinas, Thomas, 50
Aquino, Corazon, 15
Arms control theory, 87*n*.21
Augustine, St., 57
Authoritarianism, 32, 60, 73, 76, 78, 91*n*.21
Axiological approach, 55

Baltic states, 88*n*.11
Barmen Declaration, 9
Bennett, John C., 5
Berger, Peter, 3, 13, 68, 74, 89*n*.21
Bernardin, Joseph, 39
Bernardin committee, 44, 84*n*.3
Boyle, Joseph, 39
Bureaucratization, 28, 81*n*.15, 82*n*.32

Capitalism, 68
Carter, Jimmy, 13
Casaroli, Agostino, 48
Casuistry, 7
Catholicism. *See* Roman Catholic Church

Chesterton, G, K.,16
Chile, 77, 91*n*.27
China, 44, 45, 85, 86*n*.8
Christian religion, 4, 5, 35, 64. *See also specific faiths, theologies*
Communications revolution, 70–71
Communism, 23, 32, 37, 42, 46, 65, 70
Conciousness-raising, 89*n*.21
Consciencia movement, 67
Consequentialist ethics, 47
Courtney, John M., 88*n*.9
Crossman, Richard, 31

Debt crisis, 91*n*.29
Declaration of Independence, 2
Democracy, 15, 60, 75, 89*n*.19; case for, 65–71; Catholic Church and, 62; communications and, 71; definition of, 74; democratic revolutions, 14, 60, 66–68, 70; development and, 63, 68; Islam and, 89*n*.19; morality and, 61–64; Niebuhr and, 60–62; peace and, 64; policy outline, 76–77; strategic considerations, 71
Deterrence, morality and, 37–58

Development, democracy and,
63
Diamond, Larry, 69

Economic assistance programs,
68, 72
Ecumenism, 9, 10
Einstein, Albert, 24
Equality, 2

Feminism, 8
Finlandization, 38
Finnis, John, 39, 43–48, 51, 54–58,
85n.8
Foreign policy agencies, 71
Foreign policy, and morality, 1–
17

Germany, 41
Gershman, Carl, 70
Gorbachev, Mikhail, 46, 66
Green Party, 58
Grenada, 75
Grisez, G., 39
Gumbleton, Thomas, 39, 44, 84n.4
Gutierrez, Gustavo, 88n.13

Hauerwas, Stanley, 8–9
Havel, Vaclav, 14
Helsinki process, 65
Hesburgh, Thomas, 35
Hitler, A., 41
Hoffmann, Stanley, 11
Hoover Institution, 69
Houphouet-Boigny, Felix, 69
Human rights, 74
Hunthausen, Raymond, 39, 89n.4

Institute on Religion and Democ-
racy, 80n.15
Intentionality, 52
Intermediate Nuclear Force (INF)
treaty, 40
Internationalism, 5
Islamic states, 69–70, 76, 89n.19

James, Henry, 18
Japan, 68
Jefferson, Thomas, 2
Judaism, 10
Just war theory, 12, 39–40,
49

Kantian theory, 51
Kaunda, Kenneth, 69
Keegan, John, 81n.16
Kennedy, John F., 8
Koestler, Arthur, 31
Konrad, George, 14
Korea, 68, 75
Krauthammer, Charles, 3, 10
Kulturprotestantismus, 3, 4

Langan, John, 54–55
Latin America, 67, 13, 66–68,
88n.13
Leo XIII, Pope, 63
Liberal democracy, 64, 87
Liberation theology, 13, 67,
88n.13, 90n.21
Lincoln, Abraham, 2
Llosa, Mario V., 67

McNamara, Robert, 38
Malraux, Andre, 31
Man and the State (Maritain),
16
Maritain, Jacques, 16, 17
Marxism, 8, 37, 42, 46, 65, 70
Matthiesen, Leroy, 39, 85n.4
Men at Arms (Waugh), 19–22, 30
Mencken, H. L., 28
Methodist Church, 41, 85n.5
Michnik, Adam, 14
Middle East, 45
Moral Man and Immoral Society
(Niebuhr), 5
Mountbatten, L., 26
Mugabee, Robert, 69
Murray, John C., 2, 4, 6, 9, 49–50
Mutual assured destruction, 85n.5

Narco-terrorism, 66
National Association of Evangelicals, 9
National Endowment for Democracy (NED), 15, 70, 91n.27
Nationalism, 3
National security, 62
Natural law, 17, 49
Neuhaus, Richard J., 64
Niebuhr, Reinhold, 4, 5-7, 60-62, 77-78
Norms, 54
Novak, David, 10
Novak, Michael, 13, 52
Nuclear Deterrence, Morality and Realism (Finnis, Boyle, Grisez), 39, 41-43, 46, 50-56
Nuclear Non-Proliferation Treaty, 45
Nyerere, Julius, 69

O'Brian, William V., 12, 43
Officers and Gentlemen (Waugh), 22, 82n.31
Orwell, George, 32

Paul II, Pope, 63
Pax Romana, 35
Peace, 35, 91n.23; conceptions of, 56, 73; democracy and, 64, 72
Personal conscience, 53
Personalist theory, 63
Philippines, 15, 78
Pius XII, Pope, 35
Population-control policy, 91n.26
Presbyterian Church, 9, 41
Private, vs. public, 53
Protestantism, 3, 5, 9, 88n.19. *See also specific denominations; leaders*
Public, vs. private, 53

Rawlings, Jerry, 69
Rogers, Carl, 8, 42
Roh Tae Woo, 15

Roman Catholic Church: democracy and, 62; religious freedom and, 88n.19; social thought and, 84n.36; terms, 40; Waugh and, 82n.27
Rummel, R. J., 60

SDI Program, 41. *See* Strategic Defense Initiative
Segundo, Juan Luis, 91n.21
Sermon on the Mount, 10
Sexuality, 33
Silone, Ignazio, 31
Sitwell, Edith, 82n.27
Smith, Gerard, 38
Sobrino, Jon, 91n.21
Sollicitudo Rei Socialis (Pope Paul II), 63
Soviet Union, 20, 34, 38, 42-47, 55, 65, 72, 85, 86n.8. *See also* Communism
Stafford, J. Francis, 14
Stalin, Josef, 30, 34, 65
Steinfels, Peter, 88n.13
Strategic Defense Initiative (SDI), 9, 40, 41
Strategic options, 55, 71-73
Sword of Honor (Waugh), 19
Sykes, Christopher, 31, 34

Taiwan, 68
Technology, 8
Terrorism, 12
Theodicy, 60
Tillich, Paul, 34, 58
Totalitarianism, 32, 60, 72-73, 76-77
Tranquillitas Ordinis (Weigel), 56, 87n.20
Tucker, Robert, 11

Unconditional Surrender (Waugh), 22-23, 30, 33, 80n.3
Uniform Code of Military Justice, 11

Unilateralism, 44, 48, 53, 57, 84*n*.3, 85*n*.8, 86*n*.8

United States: democratization and, 71–73; foreign policy, 1–17; nationalism, 3; national security, 72, 77; universalism, 73–74. *See also specific organizations; leaders*

Universalism, 73–74

Value-free judgments, 8

Via Negitiva, 60, 65

Walzer, Michael, 11

War-decision law, 12

Waugh, Evelyn, 18–36; bureaucracy of, 81*n*.81, 82*n*.32; Catholicism of, 29, 34, 82*n*.27; democracy and, 35; on intellectuals, 83*n*.32; realism of, 82*n*.27; on sexuality, 33; totalitarianism and, 29–33; on war, 24–29, 81*n*.3

Weigel, G., 56, 85*n*.8, 87*n*.20

Wildavsky, Aaron, 15

Wilson, Woodrow, 3, 4, 76–77

Wodehouse, P. G., 18

Wohlstetter, Albert, 43

Woolsey, R. James, 9

World order theory, 13